NEGOTIATION SKILLS
FOR THE CLAIMS PROFESSIONAL

D1377546

BY

CARL VAN

(Author of <u>The 8 Characteristics of the Awesome Adjuster</u> and <u>The Claims Cookbook</u>)

AND

TERESA HEADRICK

INTERNATIONAL INSURANCE INSTITUTE, INC.

Written by Carl van Lamsweerde and Teresa Headrick
Edited by Karla Alcerro
First Edition

Copyright © 2013 International Insurance Institute, Inc.
All rights reserved.
Published by International Insurance Institute, Inc.
ISBN-10: 1480291412
ISBN-13: 9781480291416

Printed in Charleston, SC.

2112 Belle Chasse Hwy. #11-319,
Gretna, LA 70056
T: 504-393-4570
T: 888-414-8811

www.InsuranceInstitute.com

INSPIRATION

Dave Vanderpan is a friend, co-worker and business partner, whose concepts about treating people kindly and fairly are scattered throughout this book.

DEDICATION

To my step-daughter Layne Stackhouse, attorney at law, whose hard work and dedication to doing the right thing are always so impressive.

-Carl

ACKNOWLEDGEMENTS

Without the support of some key customers, we would never have had the time or opportunity to write this book. We'd like to take the time to thank these especially loyal customers for their extraordinary support.

Mike Day, Tresa Edwards – Rural Community Insurance Services

Gerry Wilson, Rick Adam– Plymouth Rock

Jill Kilroy, Twanna Amos – Horace Mann

Peter Strauss, Rick Duane, Curt Swenson - Montana State Fund

Irene Bianchi, Sandi Halpert, Mark Stewardson – RSA Insurance

Jeff Suloff – Mountain West Mutual

Michelle Gerokoulis- Electric Insurance

Jennifer Duncan, Laurel Hershman - Westfield Group

Janna Scheese, Brian Granstrand – CNA Insurance

Evelyn Jorgensen, Jamie Martin- Selective Insurance

Ken McCrea, Jennifer Boyle, Steve Rourke, Sandy VanRaalten- The Wawanesa Mutual Insurance

Andrea Bailey, Rochelle Gibson- State Comp Insurance Fund

Maria Holland, Debbie Harding-Molnar – RBC Insurance

Jon Medal, Trevor Lomberg – Northbridge Insurance

Tom Behrend, Sara Larson- Acuity

Scott Huiras, Patty Weiland- Secura Insurance

Mike Bowlin, Sandra Clarke- Cox and Palmer

Linda Adkins, Tammy Harrison, Marlene Dailey

THANK YOU

Thanks

To my daughter, Amanda van Lamsweerde, Ph.D., research psychologist, who keeps teaching me how the brain <u>really</u> works. To my step daughter, Molly Ernst-Stackhouse, fashion designer, whose determination and creativity are a constant inspiration.

-Carl

To my previous manager, and now friend, Rhonda Lindsay-Muller, who coached me to make business connections that have proved invaluable in my life, and whose business sense, natural strategic strength and personal determination inspire me daily.

-Teresa

Special Thanks

As always, a special thanks to my father, John Martin. Who not only continues to support all of my business efforts, but having raised me with a desire to help others, continues to support me with his invaluable guidance whenever I need it.

-Carl

A special thanks to my Dad, Thomas Capps, and my beautiful step mother, Mary Lou, who demonstrate to me every day how to have great enjoyment in the golden years. To my sister,

Emily Capps, for being so brave and for raising my beautiful nephew and niece. And to my step daughter, Kristi Headrick, who's diligence and spirit are so encouraging.

-Teresa

Very Special Thanks

Very special thanks to my beautiful wife, Ann van Lamsweerde, who is always there for me.

-Carl

Very special thanks to my husband, J. David Headrick, Jr., who never rolled his eyes when I said, "I am working on a book!" His support and love are vital in my life.

-Teresa

ABOUT THE AUTHOR

Carl Van was born Carl Christian Gregory Maria Baron van Lamsweerde. He was the second son of a prominent Dutch noble and artist, Franciscus Ludovicus Aloysius Maria Baron van Lamsweerde.

After the death of Carl's father at the age of 11, his mother, Joyce, married John E. Martin. Mr. Martin was a successful business owner and investor. Mr. Martin had tremendous influence over Carl, recapping stories of coming to America with virtually nothing and building a successful business. Carl admired his new father greatly, and marveled at his generosity.

Carl had a remarkable resemblance to his father Franz, and was greatly influenced by John. His mother would often comment, "I look at Carl and I see Franz. Then he starts to talk, and out comes John."

Carl worked his way through college, taking years of night school to earn his degree in Insurance. By the time he earned his degree, Carl was already a Regional Claims Manager, and even writing and teaching several IEA courses.

With his first marriage, came his daughter Amanda Elaine Denise Baroness van Lamsweerde, who Carl continuously proclaims is a child genius.

Carl married Ann Elizabeth Wimsatt, on July 16, 1994, and together they have lived in Sacramento, CA, Nashville, TN, and now reside in New Orleans, LA. In April of 1998, Carl sold his house, cashed in his retirement, and gambled it all on the idea that insurance companies would be interested in meaningful, real-life claims training. He created International Insurance Institute, Inc. a company dedicated to the enhancement of the insurance claims industry, and now widely considered the single best claims training company in the United States and Canada.

Carl Van has dedicated his life to studying how people think and interact, and has developed classes and programs to improve the success of individuals as well as business groups.

I have known Carl since we met in kindergarten, and even back then in our school days, Carl looked out for people. Obviously, Carl was honing his skills that he uses today.

It only takes a few minutes in his presence to know how passionately he believes that the greatest thing a person can do in this life, is be of service to someone in need. That, he insists, is the opportunity most of us have every single day.

In this book, Carl shares his wit, wisdom, knowledge and sixth sense of dealing with people. He's a great friend and an inspiration. I hope you find this book as valuable in your world as Carl has been in mine.

-Steve Belkin, Open All Nite Entertainment.

Professional Career

Carl Van, ITP, President & CEO of International Insurance Institute, Inc., graduated from California State University, Sacramento where he received his bachelor's degree in Insurance. He has been in the insurance claims industry since 1980 and has held the positions of Claims Adjuster, Claims Supervisor, Claims Manager, Division Claims Manager and Regional Manager over Claims, Loss Control and Premium Audit.

Mr. Van has set up 5 in-house claims training programs for various insurance companies throughout the United States, and has written articles for Claims magazine, Claims Education Magazine, Claims Advisor, Claims People magazine, The Subrogator, The National Underwriter, California Insurance Journal and has been published in over 100 other magazines. He is the author of over 75 technical and soft skill workshops being taught throughout the U.S., Canada and the U.K.

He has been a keynote speaker at claims conferences around the country, a trainer at an international U.S-Japanese executive training program, a guest speaker at hundreds of claims association seminars, and selected as the opening presenter at some of the most prestigious claims conferences in the United States and Canada.

Mr. Van is the Dean of the School of Claims Performance, and has served as both board member and Regional Vice President of the Society of Insurance Trainers and Educators where he earned his ITP designation (Insurance Training Professional).

He is owner and publisher of Claims Education Magazine, and board president of the Claims Education Conference.

Mr. Van is creator, presenter and producer of all claims training videos at Claims Education On Line, which include

Time Management, Customer Service, Negotiations and Critical Thinking, all specific to claims professionals.

He is owner and publisher of <u>Claims Professional Books On Line</u>, and is the author of the highly acclaimed book *The 8 Characteristics of the Awesome Adjuster,* which has sold internationally throughout the United States, Canada, Guam, Singapore, France, Australia, England, Chile, Ireland, and 25 other countries. Other books by Carl Van include *Gaining Cooperation, Gaining Cooperation for the Workers' Comp. Professional, The Claims Cookbook, Attitude, Ability and the 80/20 Rule* and *The Eight Characteristics of the Awesome Employee.*

Mr. Van writes all materials for his *Carl Van Claims Expert* blog, and provides claims tips on his *Carl Van Professional Speaker* You Tube channel.

Mr. Van writes all the lyrics for all songs performed by <u>Carl Van and the Awesome Adjuster Band</u>, including all 11 songs on their new CD "I'm a Claims Man."

Other credits include being an arbitrator, a licensed agent, a TASA certified expert witness for insurance Bad Faith suits, as well as a national auditor for a federal regulatory agency.

www.InsuranceInstitute.com
www.ClaimsEducationConference.com
www.CarlVan.org
www.ClaimsEducationMagazine.com
www.Facebook.com/CarlVanSpeaker
www.ClaimsEducationOnLine.com
www.Twitter.com/CarlVanSpeaker
www.ClaimsProfessionalBooks.com
www.Linkedin.com (Carl Van – Awesome Adjuster group)
www.YouTube.com/CarlVanTV
www.CarlVanClaimsExpert.wordpress.com

ABOUT THE AUTHOR

Teresa Capps Headrick was born in Chattanooga, Tennessee to Clara and Tom Capps. She grew up along with her older sister Emily in Red Bank, TN and absolutely loved the southern life. She grew up admiring Hank Aaron and Billie Jean King. As early as high school, Teresa excelled at relationship building and motivation, and built a reputation as a "people person."

Her personal life is filled with examples of her giving and caring attitude, along with her commitment to motivation and improvement through education and training. From volunteering for the American Heart Association, to her work with the Chattanooga Ronald McDonald House, Teresa revels in helping others.

Where most of us just fall into the insurance industry, Teresa seemed destined. Her mother worked at Provident Life and Accident Insurance Company as a Railroad Claims Rep. Her father's family members were all railroad employees and Provident policyholders. When Teresa's father went to downtown Chattanooga to file a Provident claim, Teresa's mother was assigned the claim. True love blossomed, and as they say, the rest is history.

Teresa began her career in insurance in 1977, steadily moved up the ranks all with the same company over an amazing 34-year career. Her managers and co-workers continuously praised her for her commitment to helping and inspiring others. She worked in multiple product lines and roles, finally moving into a training role. Her natural ability and desire to develop others and help them reach their potential made her a standout, both in the classroom and as a manager leading a busy training team.

I remember once when Teresa was selected for the Manager Spotlight in <u>Claims Education Magazine</u> (December 2009, Volume 6, Number 6). Being acutely modest, Teresa had a difficult time talking about her success, but she did admit to having a sense of humor as a central element. As she put it to the interviewer, "I am able to laugh at myself, so I am always amused." That's Teresa.

Teresa loves exercising, cooking and of course reading. Her favorite quote is by Brian Andreas, "He carried a ladder everywhere he went. After a while, people left the high places for him." These days Teresa has picked up her ladder, and is climbing high to a new adventure. She is now Director of Course Design for the International Insurance Institute.

Today, Teresa lives in Soddy Daisy, Tennessee with her husband, David, and their two dachshunds Bullet and Smokey. They are all, and I do mean all, earnest University of Tennessee football fans.

I have known Teresa since I joined her training team in 2002. Her leadership contributed to a satisfying and rewarding career for me. Her friendship and example of personal growth and development continue to enrich my life. I hope she is able to help you with her words in this book.

--- Linda Davenport

Professional Career

Teresa Headrick, ITP, CPLP, Director of Course Development, International Insurance Institute, Inc. has spent 34 years in the insurance industry, leading to management and learning/development with a staff of training consultants, quality assurance specialists and business development managers.

She has served on several strategic Leadership Councils, collaborating with other training leaders to meet the current development goals of the insurance industry.

Ms. Headrick earned her ITP (Insurance Training Professional) designation from the Society of Insurance Trainers and Educators (SITE) and her CPLP (Certified Professional in Learning and Performance) designation from the American Society for Training & Development (ASTD), specializing in Human Performance Improvement.

She has held several Board positions with the SITE, including President July 2011 – June 2012. She also served three consecutive terms as President of her regional chapter of ASTD.

Ms. Headrick has been a guest speaker at numerous insurance association meetings, and a featured instructor and course designer at the annual Claims Education Conference.

She specializes in identifying and leveraging natural talents for any size organization or team using *"StrengthsFinder 2.0 – Now, Discover Your Strengths."* She is widely considered the leading industry expert in guiding organizations on how to discover and apply strengths, putting them to work to strengthen individuals and teams.

Ms. Headrick's corporate management experience, her senior leadership roles with national and local societies, and her commitment to the insurance industry, make her uniquely qualified to write and train on the subjects of leadership and employee development.

Other credits include being a licensed insurance broker.

www.ClaimsProfessionalBooks.com
www.ClaimsEducationOnLine.com
www.ClaimsEducatonMagazine.com
www.LinkedIn.com

TABLE OF CONTENTS

INTRODUCTION
BY CARL VAN

I started International Insurance Institute, Inc. in March of 1988. From the very beginning, our <u>Negotiation Skills for Claims</u> course was one of our most popular workshops. The fact that effective negotiation is a critical skill in claims is understood by almost everyone in the insurance industry.

Now, 15 years later, our <u>Negotiation Skills for Claims</u> course is our second most popular workshop, with over 40,000 students completing the course to date. Only our <u>Awesome Claims Customer Service</u> course with over 50,000 students is more popular.

Although most of the concepts in this book are from models I have developed for our in-person workshop, I have the privilege of co-authoring this book with an incredible trainer and course designer, Teresa Headrick. If you happened to be reading something in this book, and think to yourself, "Wow, that is really profound," then that is probably Teresa's contribution.

As with many of my other books, there are going to be concepts and ideas that cross over from book to book. You may read something in here and recognize the concept from another one of my books. That is simply because the concepts I hold most true, like treating people well, cross over the different subjects so easily.

I want to make some admissions (which you will recognize right away if you have read any of my other books). Here it goes.

Admission #1: I am not a researcher. You should know that I did not conduct formal research. I have no control groups to test out my theories and no written documentation to substantiate each and every hypothesis. What I do offer is practical experience and examples to better illustrate how to negotiate effectively in claims. After 30+ years in the business world, years of management and executive experience, 15+ years of monitoring phone calls, designing training programs, and facilitating over 1,000 workshops, I have a certain perspective about what one can do to become an excellent claims negotiator. That is what I am relying upon, so don't expect to find me in some Management Journal. I'm not there. I'm here, trying to help.

Admission #2: I'm Lazy. (Probably has something to do with Admission #1) My first book, *The 8 Characteristics of the Awesome Adjuster*, was quite successful in the claims world. Ever since its release, I have been bombarded with people telling me the skills, characteristics, and attitudes that make great claims people mentioned in the book are completely transferable to almost any industry. After years of people telling me that I should rewrite it with a more general outlook, I finally agreed. That book is called, *The Eight Characteristics of the Awesome Employee.*

I dedicated quite a large section of that book to negotiating for cooperation, and decided to use some of that information for this book. Is that lazy or what?

I might be telling a story from a prior article, book, magazine, or even video presentation. I might tell the exact same story but with two different people's names. The reason for that is very simple. Sometimes I use fake names because I don't want to get sued. Would you want to get sued? No, of course you wouldn't. And neither do I. If I do make any money off of this book, I certainly don't want to spend it on legal fees defending myself against some idiot because we've used his real name in a book. So, for the most part, we will probably be using fake names.

So, if you happen to read an article I wrote a number of years ago, and we are telling that same story, and we use a different person's name, don't get your undies in a bunch. It's just what we do. So just bear with us and come along for the ride.

CHAPTER 1

WHEN THE NEGOTIATION PROCESS REALLY BEGINS

In working with claims professionals all over the world, we like to ask this question, "When does the negotiation process really begin?" Responses we hear are, "The negotiation process begins when you get the medical documentation," or "it begins when you get the reports," or "when you get the estimate from the body shop," or "when an offer is made to settle the claim." These are all good answers but we all know better, don't we?

We know the negotiation process really begins with that first conversation, that very first phone call. We know that first conversation is when we start to establish the rapport. We know that very first phone call is the foundation of the relationship that helps us towards resolution that much sooner.

A Great Place to Start

We begin learning the negotiation process by identifying what makes a great negotiator truly great. Consider this: A great negotiator is someone who.....*what*?

In many of our classes, people say, "A great negotiator is someone who listens." "A great negotiator is someone who's flexible." "A great negotiator is someone who plans things out." These are all good answers. We agree these are skills and behaviors every good negotiator should possess. So, what makes a *great* negotiator? What is it that makes them different from everybody else? Take a guess for yourself. A great negotiator is someone who....

What did you come up with? You might have guessed a great negotiator provides empathy; a great negotiator looks at things from the other person's point of view; maybe you thought a great negotiator provides a win/win solution for their customers. These are all good answers. In this book, we will share with you what makes great negotiators different from everybody else.

If you are a claims professional, you are probably doing a very good job of negotiating with your customers already. You don't need to be fixed and this book is not designed to fix you. Later, you will find the answer to the question, "What makes a great negotiator?" Using the answer, you will be able to improve yourself, develop your skills, better serve your customer and make your job easier.

A Great Negotiator is Someone Who…..

Here is the answer: A great negotiator is someone who has a process. We know this seems simple. Simple as it is, it's true.

A great negotiator is someone who has a process. You see, there are five steps to the claims negotiation process and the great negotiator uses them. They don't move onto step number two until they finish with step number one. A great negotiator doesn't get caught thinking, "Oh, uh, gee, now what do I say?" A great negotiator knows exactly what step they are in during their customer interaction. You will learn the five steps to utilize in your claim handling to improve yourself. Even if you're a good negotiator, or even if you're excellent, you can always get better. Let's get started.

CHAPTER 2

TIME SPENT NEGOTIATING

As a claims professional, you spend a lot of time negotiating. Of that time, do you know the amount of time spent negotiating the dollar amount of something? You might be surprised that only ten percent of your negotiating time is spent negotiating money. Only ten percent! The other ninety percent of the time you spend negotiating; you are actually negotiating for something else. What do you spend ninety percent of your time negotiating?

As a claims professional, you are spending ninety percent of your time negotiating for cooperation. That's right, simple cooperation. Consider this: Do you ever ask customers to sign a form and send it in? If so, you are negotiating for the customer's cooperation to move the claims process along. Do you ask customers to send in receipts? If so, you are negotiating for cooperation. Do you ask customers to return your phone call, to release a vehicle, to meet you for an inspection? The list of ways you ask customers to cooperate goes on and on. In all of these, you are negotiating for cooperation. When you ask a customer to do anything, which might be long before the claim value discussion, you're beginning a negotiation process. If they say yes, the negotiation is over. But if they say no you have to continue negotiating for their cooperation.

Remember, a great negotiator has a process and uses the same steps over and over again. You can master this first set of steps and use them every day in your job.

We will start with the three steps of negotiating for cooperation, and see how those three steps fit into our final model of the five steps of negotiating claims settlements.

As we mentioned before, when asking a customer to do something, many times the customer's answer is "yes." They cooperate and the negotiation is over. But, what if the customer's response is "no?" Let's see how a claims professional does in this example, where he asks the customer to do something, and the customer doesn't cooperate:

Mr. Drennen: "Hello."

Brad: "Yeah, Mr. Drennen, this is Brad from Typical Insurance Company. I'm calling about that medical authorization. We still haven't received that back from you yet."

Mr. Drennen: "Well, I'm not going to send it."

Brad: "What do you mean, you're not going to send it? You have to send it. I mean, we need that medical authorization."

Mr. Drennen: "I'm not signing anything. I am not sending anything."

Brad: "Well you realize, Mr. Drennen, if you don't send it, you're not getting paid."

Mr. Drennen: "I told you, Brad, I am not sending you anything. You can threaten me all you want."

Brad: "Well, I just have to remind you that your policy says you have to cooperate and if you don't, there may be no coverage at all."

Mr. Drennen: "Hey man, I'm not sending you anything."

Brad: "Well then fine, we just can't pay you."

Ultimatums Don't Pay Off

Yes, it was a little rough, but did that sound somewhat familiar? It might sound a little heavy handed, but in monitoring phone calls at different insurance companies all over the world, we can tell you, it doesn't sound too far off. Even good claims professionals, in an effort to get the customer to do something, have been heard speaking exactly like that to customers. They don't mean to be rude; they're trying to gain cooperation. However, to the customer, the ultimatum feels like being hit with a hammer.

We call this the "Claims Hammer." You know the Claims Hammer: "If you don't do this, here is the bad thing that will happen." We're trying to show the customer they should cooperate for their own benefit. Unfortunately, the words sound like a threat; it comes across as an ultimatum. Nobody likes ultimatums. Doesn't your customer deserve better?

Magic Words

As claims professionals, we know that it makes our job much easier if people trust us. You may be doing something to loose trust and you don't even realize it. The number one thing you can do to loose trust is to threaten somebody. Give somebody an ultimatum, and see if they *ever* trust you again.

On the flip side, it is very easy to earn trust. Do you know the magic word to earn trust? The magic word is "help." It's pretty easy. People trust someone who's genuinely trying to help them and they don't trust someone who's trying to hurt them.

If you say to your customer, "If you don't do this, here's what's going to happen," it can sound like a threat and destroys trust, even if you're trying to help the person. In every interaction with your customer, remember this basic rule: Offering to help earns trust.

CHAPTER 3

NEGOTIATING FOR COOPERATION – STEP ONE

STEPS TO GAINING COOPERATION:

1. WHY?
2.
3.

H ere is the situation: You ask a customer to do something and they won't cooperate. The first step to gaining their cooperation is to ask "why". We know that might seem strange to a claims professional. Why should we ask the customer, "Why" they won't cooperate? You should ask "why" because, people's reasons for not cooperating often have nothing to do with the issue at hand.

Almost always, the reason has nothing to do with the claim itself. Won't it save you time and effort if you discover the true issue by getting to the root of the customer not cooperating? Asking why can uncover the real issue and get it out of the way. Notice in the interaction in chapter 2, the claims professional, Brad, didn't ask Mr. Drennen why he wouldn't sign and send the medical authorization. In claims we are not used to asking why. We're used to just telling the customer the way it is. So, as simple as it is, or as strange as it might seem, the first step is to ask "why."

How Asking Why Works

While monitoring phone calls, we heard a claims professional, Andrea, negotiating a total loss settlement. Andrea worked hard with her customer but she missed the opportunity to ask the customer why he didn't accept her settlement figure.

Andrea had received a report indicating the customer's car was worth $12,500. She made the call to the customer, stating, "We're going to give you $12,500 for your car." The customer responds, "No way, I want $13,000." Andrea says, "Well, I have this report here that says your car is worth $12,500." The customer again responds, "I don't care, I want $13,000." At this point in the negotiation, we hear Andrea pull out the Claims Hammer. She tells the customer, "Well, sir, if you don't take the $12,500, we can't pay your rental car costs anymore." (Whack! Ouch, that hurt.)

The customer says, "It doesn't matter what you say, I still feel my car is worth $13,000." Since the customer is not hurt enough to agree, Andrea decides to hit him again with the claims hammer and says, "Sir, if you don't take the $12,500, we can't pay your storage anymore either." (Whack!)

Even though threatened again, the customer holds firm, saying, "I don't care what you say, my car is worth $13,000 and that's it." With that, Andrea tells the customer, "Well, okay. You don't have to take the $12,500, but you're the one who is still going to have to make your car payments." (Whack!)

Did you notice that not once did Andrea ask why the customer was dead-set on his car being worth $13,000?

Even though Andrea used the Claims Hammer on this customer repeatedly, she was unable to settle the case. When we heard this call, we went to speak to Andrea. We explained that if she changed her process just barely, she could have gotten the customer to agree with her. Andrea responded, "Oh, it will all work out....he'll get tired of walking."

In a way, Andrea is right. This customer is going to get tired of walking. In a week from now, this customer is going to call Andrea and say, "Okay, I'll take your $12,500, you thieves." What do you think the customer has done during the last week? He's complained: he's complained to our agent, he's made complaints about Andrea and the claims process, and he's told every single person that he's met at every party how horrible the company is.

In this case, we did something we almost never do - we actually called the customer. We told the customer we were monitoring the call for quality assurance and asked the customer why he felt his car was worth $13,000. You know, the answer to that question had nothing to do with any report of evaluation. It had nothing to do with rental charges, or with storage fees, or even car payments. The reason this customer wanted $13,000 had <u>nothing</u> to do with what Andrea was beating him to pieces with. Andrea just didn't know it, because she never asked why.

Do you know what the customer told us? He said, "Look, my brother died about six months ago and he gave me this car. The car means a lot to me. I know you're going to say it doesn't mean anything to you but it does to me. You know what, somebody had offered him $13,000 for this car and I'm not going to let you rip him off."

Given what that customer told us, do you think he is going to be swayed by any of the threats that Andrea leveled at him? No, because they aren't important to him. This customer was convinced if he took one penny less than $13,000, he has let an insurance company rip off his dead brother. He's not going to be swayed by anything Andrea was pounding on him with.

Andrea thought her process of using the Claims Hammer on the customer, hitting him with reasons to "give in", was effective. Andrea was not successful because she never asked the customer why. Andrea's process wasted her time and effort. Let's see how we can improve Andrea's process.

Getting What You Asked For

When a great negotiator asks a customer to do something and the customer says no, the first thing he/she does is to ask "why." When asked why, the customer responds with their reasons.

You might say, "Okay, you told me to ask why and I did. Now, I am getting really weird reasons." Notice in Andrea's case, the reason the customer wanted $13,000 had nothing to do with the value of the car. Nevertheless, Andrea's customer, and every customer, has a right to their reasons.

Even though you know the customer has a right to their reasons, you might catch yourself working to convince the customer how wrong those reasons are. But great negotiators never argue with reasons. You could be tempted to persuade the customer to forget their reasons and "give in" to your offer. Great negotiators never do that. They do something very different. What is it?

CHAPTER 4

NEGOTIATING FOR COOPERATION – STEP TWO

STEPS TO GAINING COOPERATION:

1. WHY?
2. ACKNOWLEDGE
3.

Any great negotiator can tell that there is no point in talking if nobody is listening. One of the most important skills any claims professional can possess is the ability to get customers to listen to his/her point of view.

Throughout this book we will review the five claims negotiation maxims that have been developed specifically for claims professionals. The first one has to do with getting people to listen to what you have to say.

Maxim #1: People will consider your point of view to the exact degree you have demonstrated you understand their point of view. (See figure 4.1)

Figure 4.1

Carl Van's Claims Negotiation Maxims

The most important thing to remember when negotiating the settlement of any claim is that we are in the customer service business. We are in the business of helping people. Even if someone does not get everything they want, as long as they still feel they were treated with respect by a knowledgeable professional, who cares about doing a good job, they may just be satisfied.

Claims Maxim #1: **People will consider your point of view to the exact degree you have demonstrated you understand their point of view.** (Listen! Then paraphrase back what you hear)

These claims negotiation maxims were developed by Carl Van for the book *Gaining Cooperation* and the workshop *Negotiation Skills for Claims Professionals* and copyrighted © 1999, 2001, 2003 – 2013. They are specific to the training offered by International Insurance Institute, and may not be used by any other person or entity in connection with any training or document without the express written permission of International Insurance Institute, Inc.

Step #2 of the negotiating for cooperation process is to "acknowledge". This acknowledgement step is simply to let the other person know that you understand their point of view. You are <u>not</u> telling them that they are right. You are <u>not</u> telling them you agree with them. You are simply letting them know that you appreciate their point of view.

Let's take a look at Brad using the acknowledgement step, but not getting anywhere with Mr. Drennen:

Mr. Drennen: "Hello."

Brad: "Hello, Mr. Drennen, this is Brad with Typical Insurance Company. I'm calling about that medical authorization we sent you a while back. We still haven't received that signed."

Mr. Drennen: "Well, Brad, that's because I haven't signed it and I haven't sent it."

Brad: "Well, can I ask you why?"

Mr. Drennen: "Yeah, my neighbor, who is in his second year of law school, told me, don't sign anything. Don't send anything."

Brad: "Well, Mr. Drennen, to get your medical bills paid for, you need to actually sign that, send it back, or we can't pay your claim."

Mr. Drennen: "But I just told you, Brad, my neighbor is in his second year of law school, he said, don't sign anything, don't send them anything."

Brad: "If you don't sign it, you might not even have coverage because you are not cooperating under the terms of the policy, so you need to sign that and send it back to us."

Mr. Drennen: "I don't think you're listening to me, Brad. I just told you, that's exactly what my neighbor told me not to do. So, I'm not going to do it."

Brad: "Mr. Drennen, you know if you don't sign the medical authorization, you're going to have to pay those bills yourself. We won't be able to pay them."

Did you see what happened in this case? Brad does ask Mr. Drennen why he won't cooperate and was clearly given the reason. In order to take the high road, in order to not argue with Mr. Drennen's reasons, Brad totally ignored them. Brad works hard not to rock the boat and move straight to the facts. Unfortunately, Mr. Drennen must feel completely ignored.

The problem with that is we're in a negotiating process, aren't we? During the negotiating process, is it a good idea to completely ignore the points and reasons a customer gives us? Is that a good negotiation technique? Probably not.

Great negotiators listen. In this case, Brad listened, but he totally ignored what he learned.

Let's take a look at another pitfall that Brad and many claims professionals might fall into. Pay attention to what Brad can do better. Right now the only thing we know how to do is ask why. We are not quite to Step Two yet. Here's the interaction:

Mr. Drennen: "Hello."

Brad: "Hello, Mr. Drennen, this is Brad from Typical Insurance Company. I'm calling about that medical authorization. We still haven't received that from you yet."

Mr. Drennen: "Yeah, that's because I haven't sent it."

Brad: "Can I ask you why not?"

Mr. Drennen: "Well my neighbor is in his second year of law school. He told me, don't sign anything, and don't send anything."

Brad: "Second year of law school, what does that have to do with anything? I mean, where are you getting your advice anyway? You've got to sign that authorization, send it back to me so we can pay your medical bills."

Mr. Drennen: "Well he's in law school, he said, don't sign anything, and don't send anything."

Brad: "Well, you're getting some bad information, because, you know what, if you don't send that back, we're not going to pay your claim. And besides, you have to cooperate under your policy."

At least, Brad is trying. Unfortunately, he did what many of us might do. Brad argued. He argued with the customer's reason. Unfortunately, that doesn't work very well. We now need to introduce our next claims negotiation maxim.

Maxim #2: Great claims negotiators never argue with reasons, they argue the facts. (See figure 4.2)

Figure 4.2

Carl Van's Claims Negotiation Maxims

The most important thing to remember when negotiating the settlement of any claim is that we are in the customer service business. We are in the business of helping people. Even if someone does not get everything they want, as long as they still feel they were treated with respect by a knowledgeable professional, who cares about doing a good job, they may just be satisfied.

Claims Maxim #1: **People will consider your point of view to the exact degree you have demonstrated you understand their point of view.** (Listen! Then paraphrase back what you hear)

Claims Maxim #2: **Great claims negotiators never argue with reasons, they argue the facts.** (Acknowledge their reasons and move on)

These claims negotiation maxims were developed by Carl Van for the book *Gaining Cooperation* and the workshop *Negotiation Skills for Claims Professionals* and copyrighted © 1999, 2001, 2003 – 2013. They are specific to the training offered by International Insurance Institute, and may not be used by any other person or entity in connection with any training or document without the express written permission of International Insurance Institute, Inc.

In Brad's case, when he said, *"Well, you're getting some bad information..."* he was trying to convince Mr. Drennen that talking to his neighbor was the wrong thing to do. Guess how this automatically sounds to the customer? To Mr. Drennen, this is an attack on his neighbor. This is not smart because Mr. Drennen already trusts his neighbor more than he trusts Brad.

Can a claims professional get any more off track? Unfortunately, yes. As soon as Brad criticizes the neighbor, he's not even really attacking the neighbor. You know who he's attacking? He's attacking Mr. Drennen for relying on the neighbor.

At this point, Brad's customer may never cooperate, no matter how much Brad negotiates. Do you know why? Because Mr. Drennen would have to admit that his trust in his neighbor was misplaced and that he was wrong.

We know it is unlikely our customers can be convinced they are wrong and to totally change their mind. How do you avoid this entirely? "Acknowledge" their point of view so you can get back to talking about the facts.

Remember, we're not saying we agree with the customer, we're not saying they're right. We're simply saying, "I understand your point of view." If you want customers to be reasonable, the best thing you can do is let them know, "I already think you're reasonable."

Many claims professionals take the approach, "Let me show you how wrong you are." Great negotiators never argue with reasons; they argue the facts.

In this case, the customer had his reason. Right or wrong, the customer isn't signing the medical authorization form because his neighbor told him not to. Notice, the reason has nothing to do with the fact that we need this form signed under the provisions of the policy, it's just the reason. Great negotiators know it's a waste of time and effort to argue with reasons; they only argue the facts.

Great negotiators listen and they trust their process to gain cooperation during negotiations. Step one is to ask "why," step two is to "acknowledge" the customers reasons. After hearing the reason, Brad can move toward gaining cooperation from Mr. Drennen. Let's see how he does this time.

Mr. Drennen: "Hello."

Brad: "Hello, Mr. Drennen, this is Brad from Typical Insurance Company. I'm calling about that medical authorization. We still haven't received that from you yet."

Mr. Drennen: "Yeah, that's because I haven't sent it."

Brad: "Can I ask you why not?"

Mr. Drennen: "Well my neighbor is in his second year of law school. He told me, don't sign anything, and don't send anything."

Brad: "Mr. Drennen, I can appreciate that. If you have talked to your neighbor, who is someone you respect and trust, and he told you not to sign anything, it's totally reasonable that you may not want to sign and send that form back."

With a few simple words, you can prove to the customer that you were listening, and whether you agree or not, you can appreciate the reasons why the customer isn't cooperating. It may take practice for you to acknowledge the customer's response to "why" without arguing. It's worth the effort as that simple demonstration of understanding earns you more than you can imagine.

How Acknowledgement Makes Your Job Easier

All over the world, claims professionals tell us their jobs would be easier if the customer would just listen to them. Do you agree? We even imagine Brad would agree that his job would be easier if Mr. Drennen would just listen to him.

Step #2, acknowledging the customer's point of view or reasons for not cooperating can be a statement as simple as, *"If those are your reasons, I appreciate that. Here's what we have to do."* Until the customer hears this acknowledgment, he probably isn't listening to you.

Trying to prove to the customer that their reasons are wrong makes your job very difficult. It is an impossible task to convince the customer to admit they were wrong and to change their mind. That's not what we want to do. What we want to do is acknowledge their point of view so we can get back to talking about the facts. Remember, we are here to provide customer service and not win arguments.

Removing the But

There is one very important thing we want to mention regarding the acknowledgement step. If all you do in the acknowledgement step is to say, "Yeah <u>but</u>..." or "Yeah I understand that <u>but</u>..." it will not work. Remember that we said people will consider your point of view to the exact degree you have demonstrated you understand their point of view. So, what does that mean? That means you really have to prove to the customer you understand them. What's the best way to let someone know you understand their point of view? Repeat it back to them. Actually say it back to them as Brad does:

> *Brad: "Mr. Drennen, I can appreciate that. If you have talked to your neighbor, who is someone you respect and trust, and he told you not to sign anything, it's totally reasonable that you may not want to sign and send that form back."*

Great negotiators acknowledge the customer's reasons as sensible without a "but" to get them to change their mind.

Listen Up

The acknowledgement step is very powerful and there's a skill that is vital to your success in using it – listening. You might catch yourself saying to a customer, "Look, if the reason you don't want to sign this form is because... because... why don't you want to sign this form again?" Guess what that proves to you? It proves you weren't listening.

We find that claims professionals believe the facts are what convince their customers to cooperate. However, we believe it's not the facts that convince people, it's getting them to have an <u>open</u> <u>mind</u> to consider your facts. How can you achieve that? By demonstrating you understand their point of view. Did you notice how Brad acknowledged Mr. Drennen's reason? Brad fully demonstrated he understood the customer's point of view by repeating the reason back and then saying, "That's perfectly reasonable." Remember, if you aren't listening you won't be able to accomplish this. Also remember, to just say, "Well, yes, <u>but,</u>" will not work.

Once you have mastered using step two, you are ready to move on to step three.

CHAPTER 5

NEGOTIATING FOR COOPERATION – STEP THREE

STEPS TO GAINING COOPERATION:

1. WHY?
2. ACKNOWLEDGE
3. FACTS

S tep three is to get back to talking about the facts. We said a customer's reasons may have nothing to do with the facts of their case but those reasons become obstacles for the customer to <u>hear</u> the facts. You can quickly move beyond the obstacle and get what you are asking for when you acknowledge a customer's reasons for not cooperating. You have their attention and they are now ready to listen to you.

Let's go back and see how Brad moves on to the facts after the acknowledgement step:

Mr. Drennen: "Hello."

Brad: "Hello, Mr. Drennen, this is Brad from Typical Insurance Company. I'm calling about that medical authorization. We still haven't received that from you yet."

Mr. Drennen: "Yeah, that's because I haven't sent it."

Brad: "Can I ask you why not?"

Mr. Drennen: "Well my neighbor is in his second year of law school. He told me, don't sign anything, and don't send anything."

Brad: "Mr. Drennen, I can appreciate that. If you have talked to your neighbor, who is someone you respect and trust, and he told you not to sign anything, it's totally reasonable that you may not want to sign and send that form back."

Mr. Drennen: "Right."

Brad: "The purpose of this form is to allow us to get your medical information so we can pay you. If you sign the form and send it to me, I'll get busy gathering

your information to process your claim; and if you
want to run that by your neighbor, I am fine with that."

Mr. Drennen: "Hmm. Well, fine."

How do you think Brad did? Definitely better. In a matter of seconds, Brad has gotten to the root of the delay in receiving the signed form, acknowledged the reason without attacking the customer, and clearly stated the facts. Very quickly, Brad asked why, acknowledged Mr. Drennen's point of view, and got back to talking about the facts.

Remember what we said before, most of the time, a customer's reason for not cooperating has <u>nothing</u> to do with the issue at hand. What you don't have to do is prove the customer wrong. That leads us into our next claims negotiation maxim.

Maxim #3- You never have to prove anyone wrong; you only have to prove yourself right. (See Figure 5.1)

Most people believe that the best way to change someone's mind is to show that they are wrong. We would like to submit at this point that the very best claims people don't bother trying to get a customer to admit or believe they are wrong. The best claims people spend time showing the customer that they are right.

The problem with trying to either convince someone or get someone to admit that they are wrong so that they can change their mind, is that there are some people who will never admit that they are wrong. Do you know anybody like this?

They see "wrong" as the same word as "stupid". Therefore, they will never admit that they are wrong, because to them, that would mean admitting they are stupid. Why work that hard? We already have a tough job in claims. Don't bother trying to prove anyone wrong; just focus on proving yourself right.

Figure 5.1

Carl Van's Claims Negotiation Maxims

The most important thing to remember when negotiating the settlement of any claim is that we are in the customer service business. We are in the business of helping people. Even if someone does not get everything they want, as long as they still feel they were treated with respect by a knowledgeable professional, who cares about doing a good job, they may just be satisfied.

Claims Maxim #1: **People will consider your point of view to the exact degree you have demonstrated you understand their point of view.** (Listen! Then paraphrase back what you hear)

Claims Maxim #2: **Great claims negotiators never argue with reasons, they argue the facts.** (Acknowledge their reasons and move on)

Claims Maxim #3: **You never have to prove anyone wrong, you only have to prove yourself right.** (No one likes to be wrong, so don't waste your time)

So the steps to gain cooperation are:

Step 1: Ask why
Step 2: Acknowledge the customer's point of view
Step 3: Get back to talking about the facts

We know it may take practice for you to successfully use this process to gain cooperation. Let's take a look at another interaction that can help you learn. Remember the three steps, *why, acknowledge, facts,* and see where Laura falters with the customer:

Mr. Tony: "Hello."

Laura: "Hello, Mr. Tony, this is Laura from Typical Insurance Company. I'm calling about the Proof of Loss we sent you. We still haven't received that signed and returned to us yet."

Mr. Tony: "Yeah, I've decided not to sign it."

Laura: "Can I ask you why not?"

Mr. Tony: "Sure. The first person I talked to at your company told me I didn't have to sign anything."

Laura: "Who told you that?"

Mr. Tony: "I don't remember names. You're like the fifth person that's called me."

Laura: "Well, I recognize that we have had a lot of turnover. We have a lot of new people. But I can't imagine anybody telling you that you wouldn't have to sign anything. We need that in order to set up your claim."

Mr. Tony: "You guys have got to get your stories straight."

As you can tell, Laura fell into the old trap of arguing with a customer's reasons. We don't have to work this hard; yet, many times we do. Knowing the three steps for gaining cooperation, what would you have said differently?
Let's look at the exact same scenario, this time with the right steps applied:

Mr. Tony: "Hello."

Laura: "Hello, Mr. Tony, this is Laura from Typical Insurance Company. I'm calling about the Proof of Loss we sent you. We still haven't received that signed."

Mr. Tony: "Yeah, I've decided not to sign it."

Laura: "Can I ask you why not?"

Mr. Tony: "Sure. The first person I talked to at your company told me I didn't have to sign anything."

Laura: "Mr. Tony, if you were told you wouldn't have to sign anything, then I can certainly understand why you wouldn't want to. That's reasonable. I apologize that someone gave you the wrong information. As a matter of fact, by completing the Proof of Loss, it will allow me to get your claim set up. The sooner you sign the form and return it to me, the sooner I can get moving on your claim, and hopefully help you get it resolved just that much quicker."

Mr. Tony: "Well, ok, fine, but you guys have to get your stories straight."

Laura: "Again, I apologize. I'll be looking forward to getting that from you."

Mr. Tony: "Alright, let me work on it."

This is a much more efficient and effective process in gaining cooperation from the customer. In claims, we don't have to argue with customers and prove them wrong, as much as we think we do. It's <u>much</u> easier to convince the customer that we're right, rather than proving them wrong.

In the next chapter, we discuss skills that will help you not only when negotiating claims, but with all interactions with customers.

CHAPTER 6

LISTENING FOR EMOTIONAL WORDS

C arl was monitoring phone calls and heard this exact call. As you read the interaction, consider if you were faced with this situation, and knowing the three steps, how you would respond to the customer. Here's the actual interaction (with the names changed) that Carl heard:

Mr. Swope: "Hello."

Meg: "Hello, this is Meg from Typical Insurance Company and I'm calling about your auto accident. I know you had damage to your car. I am sorry that we don't have any independent adjusters available right now. Can you get the estimate on the repairs and send that to me?"

Mr. Swope: "No way, I'm not going to do that."

Meg: "Why is that?"

Mr. Swope: "I'll tell you why. Because I'm the victim here. Why should I run around doing your job?"

Meg: "Well, it's not my job to prove your claim, it's your job and you have to do this in order to…… " and Meg launched into the facts.

How would you have dealt with Mr. Swope? You know you don't want to argue, and you need to demonstrate you understand his point of view, so he will be open to hearing the facts. But, what is Mr. Swope really telling Meg?

When Mr. Swope responded, "Because I'm the victim here", Meg missed the highly emotional word – victim – and started arguing about whose job it was. Here is our suggestion: pay special attention when customers use emotional words. They are vivid and, if you are listening, are easy to pick out during the conversation.

When customers use emotional words with their reasons, it is probably a hint that this issue is important to them. In this case, Mr. Swope used the word "victim". What do we normally associate the word victim with? We associate victim with a crime. Mr. Swope is actually using the word as if he was the victim of a crime. And you know what? He's not too far off. Mr. Swope wasn't doing anything wrong when his car was slammed into. Now, <u>he</u> has to miss a day of work running around getting estimates for the repairs. No wonder Mr. Swope feels like a victim. It's perfectly reasonable.

The Empathic Connection

Think of the empathic connection as the difference between what someone said and what they meant. Consider what Mr. Swope said – "I'm the victim here." What Mr. Swope wanted is empathy for being involved in a car accident. What Meg should have done is focus on the emotional word and what it meant. This is the ability to make an empathic connection. That's not always easy.

Here's another example that Carl heard while monitoring phone calls. The claims professional was talking to a customer and the customer said, "Oh man, my brand new Porsche is creamed." The adjuster said, "Don't worry, we'll compensate you for the repairs." It's subtle but the customer is asking for empathy that his brand new Porsche has been creamed. The claims professional missed what was meant –vs. - what was said.

Try this one. Let's say a wife walks up to her husband and says, "Wow, Shirley sure is lucky her husband brings <u>her</u> flowers." The husband responds, "She sure is." Obviously, what the wife said and what she meant are two different things. What did she mean when she said, "Shirley sure is lucky her husband brings her flowers"? She meant, "I would like flowers, please." But that's not what she <u>said</u>. The poor husband didn't make the empathic connection between what the wife said and what she really meant.

Let's go back to the customer with the Porsche. The claims professional didn't make the empathic connection either. When the customer said, "My brand new Porsche is creamed," the customer wasn't asking, "Will I be compensated for the damages to my automobile?" That's not at all what the customer was saying. What the customer was saying was, "My life is upside down right now. I am so upset, I'm beside myself."

If the claims professional had considered what was meant vs. what was said and made the empathic connection, the adjuster could have said something like, "You know what, if your brand new Porsche is creamed, I am sorry. I know this is going to be difficult for you. I know you probably loved that car and if there was a way I could take that accident back, I'd love to do it. I just can't. What I <u>can</u> do is to make sure you get everything you're entitled to."

As a claims professional, you should listen for emotional words and consider what the customer means. A genuine, empathic connection with the customer is a skill that great negotiators use to gain cooperation in what they are asking.

Great negotiators take their empathic connection a step further; they tie in the customer changing the way they feel, to what they want the customer to do. If you can tie in the customer changing the way they feel, with what you want them to do, the more likely the customer will do it.

Here's an example of what we mean:

> *Mr. Swope: "Hello."*
>
> *Meg: "Hello, this is Meg from Typical Insurance Company and I'm calling about your auto accident. I know you had damage to your car. I am sorry that we don't have any independent adjusters available right now. Can you get the estimate on the repairs and send that to me?"*

Mr. Swope: "No way, I'm not going to do that."

Meg: "Why is that?"

Mr. Swope: "I'll tell you why. Because I'm the victim here. Why should I run around doing your job?"

Meg: "You know, Mr. Swope, if you don't want to get an estimate because you're feeling like a victim, I can understand that. You weren't doing anything wrong and our insured slammed into you. I appreciate how this makes you feel. I'll tell you what, if you can go get an estimate, some good things will happen. First of all, you will get to pick the shop and you can pick someone you trust. Second, you'll be there when they write the estimate to make sure they don't miss anything and that's good for you. And third, if you can get them to fax it to me, I'll get a check out to you as soon as possible. When you're back on the road and can get all of this behind you, maybe you won't have to feel like a victim anymore. Because that's a lousy way to feel and I'd like to help."

Did you see how Meg acknowledged Mr. Swope's reason, made the empathic connection of what was meant with the emotional word, and tied in getting what she wanted from him? Maybe Mr. Swope will do what Meg asks, and maybe he won't. Either way, Meg's job is hard enough without arguing with Mr. Swope about whether or not he's a victim or whose job it is to prove his claim.

If you bought new power tools, you would read the instructions, right? In the next chapter, we continue to learn from interactions in gaining cooperation from customers. These processes and skills are your new power tools.

CHAPTER 7

POWER TOOLS: YOUR PROCESS AND SKILLS

U sing the three step process, listening for emotional words, and making the empathic connection while asking for what you want, will help you gain cooperation from your customer. This is where you spend 90% of your negotiating time; isn't it worth practicing?

Here's another interaction, a bit harder this time, to help you learn. As a claims professional, you might have heard this from customers before. See if you can determine what goes wrong and consider what you would have said instead:

Ms. Craig: "Hello."

Stan: "Yes, hello, Ms. Craig, this is Stan from Typical Insurance Company. I'm calling to get a recorded statement from you regarding your claim."

Ms. Craig: "No way, I'm not doing that."

Stan: "Well, you need to. In order for us to handle your claim and for you to get paid, you need to give us your recorded statement."

Ms. Craig: "Well, I want to get paid."

Stan: "Well then, you need to give that statement to us now."

Ms. Craig: "No."

Stan: "Well, I mean, if you don't do it, obviously we can't process your claim. We won't know who's at fault for the accident."

We hope you are thinking you would have asked Ms. Craig why. Let's say Ms. Craig would have responded with something like, "Because you will just use it against me." In the past, the first thing that may have jumped into your head is to argue with Ms. Craig to prove her wrong. Now, we hope, you are considering how to acknowledge Ms. Craig's point of view instead of arguing with her reasons.

Remember, you're not saying you think Ms. Craig is right. You're not saying you agree with Ms. Craig. You are simply expressing, "I appreciate your point of view." We hope you remember how to best demonstrate you understand Ms. Craig's reasons. It is to repeat back what she said. In this case, Ms. Craig has pretty good reasons, so how can you acknowledge her point of view and get back to the facts?

Here's our suggestion on how Stan can demonstrate he thinks Ms. Craig is reasonable, then get back to the facts:

> *Ms. Craig: "Hello."*
>
> *Stan: "Yes, hello, Ms. Craig, this is Stan from Typical Insurance Company. I'm calling to get a recorded statement from you regarding your claim."*
>
> *Ms. Craig: "No way, I'm not doing that."*
>
> *Stan: "Can I ask why?"*
>
> *Ms. Craig: "Because you will just use it against me."*
>
> *Stan: "Ms. Craig, if you don't want to give me a recorded statement, because you're concerned that we're going to use it against you, I appreciate that. That makes sense. My goal is not to use this against you. I know there are always two sides to every story and you are entitled to have your say. If you allow me to take your*

recorded statement, I can consider your version of the accident and get busy processing this claim."

What do you think? Is Ms. Craig more likely to cooperate with what Stan is asking? Stan actually demonstrates "I appreciate your point of view AND we're just trying to do the right thing." Stan uses no energy arguing with Ms. Craig's reasons.

To review, if you want your customer to be reasonable, demonstrate to them you already think they are being reasonable.

As we learned in chapter 2, one of the hallmarks of really great customer service providers is they use the word "help" quite a bit. In claims, we can use this power. Why? As we said before, customers will trust someone to the degree they are being helped.
This leads us into Claims Maxim #4.

Maxim #4: People trust someone who is trying to help them and don't trust someone who is trying to hurt them.
(See figure 7.1)

Consider these examples:

Don't Say	Say
"If you don't sign this form, we can't pay your workers' comp. benefits."	*"If you do sign this form, we can help get your workers' comp. benefits paid."*
"We're going to take depreciation on your roof."	*"Let me help explain why we are going to take depreciation."*
"It sounds like you're confused."	*"Perhaps I can help by explaining this more clearly."*
"If you don't release your vehicle, you will get stuck with the fees."	*"If you do release your vehicle, I can help you avoid unnecessary fees."*

The positive phrase is a very powerful tool for claims people. It will take practice to remove the "don't, won't, and can't" words from your vocabulary. The very next interaction you have with a customer, tell them you will help, and lead with what you CAN do. You have the power to earn the customer's trust.

Here's another interaction between a customer and a claims professional. We want you to determine what goes wrong and what you might say instead:

Ken: "Hello."

Karen: "Hello, Ken, this is Karen from Typical Insurance Company. I'm calling about your home owner claim. I need you to send in the receipts for the property that you have replaced."

Ken: "Well, Karen, I don't want to do that."

Karen: "Can I ask you why not, Ken?"

Ken: "Well, yeah, because I'm not ready to settle the claim yet."

Karen: "Yeah, well anyway, you need to send us those receipts."

Ken: "I know Karen, but I told you, I'm not going to do it because I'm not ready to settle."

Karen: "Well, you realize that without receipts, I can't pay you anything."

Ken: "Karen, I don't want to send them in yet."

Karen: "Ken, you don't seem to understand. By not sending them in, it will only delay the claim. You have got to send them in."

Ken: "Karen, let me tell you clearly, I don't want to."

You know, this customer has good reasons for not cooperating: "Well, yeah, because I'm not ready to settle the claim yet." For those of you in the homeowner industry, you likely have heard this from customers, and you know it is not true that sending in the receipts means being ready to settle the entire claim. You might previously have argued and corrected the customer. Regardless of your industry, you now know a better way to negotiate with Ken for his cooperation because you have tools and the proven three steps: ***why, acknowledge, facts***. Let's see Karen put this to work with her customer:

Ken: "Hello."

Karen: "Hello, Ken, this is Karen from Typical Insurance Company. I'm calling about your home owner claim. I need you to send in the receipts for the property that you have replaced."

Ken: "Well, Karen, I don't want to do that."

Karen: "Can I ask you why not, Ken?"

Ken: "Well, yeah, because I'm not ready to settle the claim yet."

Karen: "I can appreciate if you're not ready to settle and that you think sending in receipts means that you have to settle now. Ken, I assure you, that's not the case. It doesn't mean that you can't settle later. It just means that, by sending your receipts now, I can get busy justifying the value of your claim, which will make things go much quicker when you are ready. Does that sound alright?"

Ken: "I guess. Alright, fine."

Did Karen argue? No. Did Karen waste any energy? No. Did Karen gain cooperation? Yes. Remember, 90% of the time you spend negotiating, you're negotiating for cooperation, so continue to practice your power tools and the three step process.

Figure 7.1

Carl Van's Claims Negotiation Maxims

The most important thing to remember when negotiating the settlement of any claim is that we are in the customer service business. We are in the business of helping people. Even if someone does not get everything they want, as long as they still feel they were treated with respect by a knowledgeable professional, who cares about doing a good job, they may just be satisfied.

Claims Maxim #1: **People will consider your point of view to the exact degree you have demonstrated you understand their point of view.** (Listen! Then paraphrase back what you hear)

Claims Maxim #2: **Great claims negotiators never argue with reasons, they argue the facts.** (Acknowledge their reasons and move on)

Claims Maxim #3: **You never have to prove anyone wrong, you only have to prove yourself right.** (No one likes to be wrong, so don't waste your time)

Claims Maxim #4: **People trust someone who is trying to help them and don't trust someone who is trying to hurt them.** (Put away the Claims Hammer for a moment)

At the Root of Your Success

We talked about listening in chapter 4; you must listen to be able to repeat back what the customer said. Listening is a critical skill at the root of your negotiating success.

How critical is it? In our negotiation classes, we ask claims people to finish this sentence: My job as a claims professional would be so much easier if customers would just _____.

Consistently, the top answer is "listen". Oh, if customers would just listen. We want to let you in on a secret that we have learned while monitoring phone calls. There are a lot of arguments heard while listening to claims phone calls but that's not the secret. The secret is that most arguments are started by the claims person who didn't hear what the customer just said – and we mean what they *just* said.

You are in control of your ability to listen to customers. Eliminate all distractions while you work with them. They deserve your full attention and will know when you give it to them. Do this on every call, with every customer and reduce the chance of arguments that derail your successful negotiations.

To demonstrate another benefit of listening to the customer, see if you can tell the difference between the following two statements:

"I really think my claim is worth $10,000 and you should pay me $10,000 now."

"I really feel my claim is worth $10,000 and you should pay me $10,000 now."

What is the difference? The difference is one customer says "think" and one says "feel". It is a subtle difference that makes a big difference in how you work with your customer.

It may be easy to conclude that people who use the word "think" in common conversation to describe their beliefs are typically more analytical. They gravitate more towards factual information that we give them and they pick up on that information pretty quickly. So, if you are talking about the nuts and bolts of the claim, you will probably be on the same page with the customer. That doesn't mean that people who are analytical, or typically use the word "think" in common conversation, will settle every claim for the very first amount that you offer. It's not that easy, but you can typically start talking about the facts much more quickly.

On the other hand, it is also easy to conclude that people, who use the word "feel" in common conversation to describe their beliefs, typically have more of an emotional tie to what they are saying. You've really got to pay attention to the customer who says, "I really feel my claim is worth..." If not, you will be moving forward to give the factual information about their claim, and the customer is more tied up in the emotional aspect. Give the customer your attention and acknowledgement of their emotional tie before you get to the facts.

Being able to listen effectively to those cues will help you negotiate that much more effectively going forward.

Are you ready to go on and learn more of what great negotiators know? In addition to the tools, skills and the three step process, there are three critical factors for all claims professionals to be great at negotiations.

CHAPTER 8

THREE IMPORTANT FACTORS FOR A SUCCESSFUL NEGOTIATION

Important Factor #1 - Knowledge

Claims knowledge is absolutely critical. We work very hard to build our skills, our expertise over our careers, and we do a good job of investigating files, going to classes, taking on-line seminars, learning things day by day that make us better at what we do. Having knowledge is critical because knowledge is confidence.

We came across an adjuster who told us, "I really don't know if I'm capable of handling this file. The attorney is asking for $100,000. I don't think that I should negotiate this claim. I need to reassign it to somebody else."

When asked, "How well do you know your file?" the adjuster quickly responded, "I know it really well. You know, I looked at the police report. I investigated the file. I talked to all the parties. I took the statements. I looked at the photos of the vehicles."

When asked, "How confident are you in your evaluation?" the adjuster again quickly responded, "Compared to other cases that I have evaluated that are similar, this one seems to be in-line. I think it's where it needs to be."

So, what is shaking this adjuster's confidence in calling the attorney? Very simply, the adjuster had never had a case where an attorney had asked for $100,000. We said, "But you know the case, and knowledge is power."

When you enter into a negotiation, having confidence is absolutely critical. By having knowledge of the file, the other side will feel your confidence. On the flip-side, they'll sense if you're not confident going into the conversation. If you go into that conversation saying, "Well, you know, I think I can offer you something around $5,000", they're going to sense the fact that you sound timid and scared. They will probably take advantage of it.

Claims knowledge is your first important factor and earns you two benefits: It builds your self-confidence to pick up the phone and enter into a conversation feeling "I can do this." It also gives confidence to the other side that they are having a conversation with a professional who really does know their file. When they realize you're a true claims professional, they are much more likely to listen and take heart in the things you say.

Knowledge is power for claims professionals.

Important Factor #2 - Empathy

There is never a bad time for empathy. As you learned earlier when we introduced empathy during the "acknowledgement" step, expressing empathy in their situation establishes a willingness for the customer to actually cooperate with what you want them to do.

Very simply, empathy is expressing that you know where the customer is coming from. People love to know they are being heard and the way to do that is by acknowledging what they said with an empathic statement. Here are some examples of empathic statements:

"I understand this is important to you."

"I know this is a tough circumstance."

"I'm sorry you have to go through this."

After using an empathic statement, be very careful not to say "but" or "however". If you say "but" or "however", it removes all importance from your empathic statement and tells the customer you really did not mean it. Saying "but" and "however" when we have more to say is a habit that takes work to break. Make your empathic statement really stick: just put a period after what you said, take a breath and move on with your next statement or your next phrase.

Empathy is top priority for claims professionals.

Important Factor #3 - Communication

Experts tell us, of all communications, the *spoken* word is approximately 40% of the entire message or conversation. The other 60% of communication is non-verbal. That is extremely important for us to understand and realize how non-verbal communication impacts our efforts to negotiate.

If you are in a claims position where you meet customers in person, have you watched them look away in disinterest? Have you observed slumped posture? Have you seen somebody rolling their eyes when they are talking to you? Are they folding their arms in a very defensive manner? These are all signs, clear non-verbal messages the customer is sending you during the communication process.

For those of you who handle claims on the phone, you don't have the benefit of seeing non-verbal signs by the customer. Can the customer really tell if you are disinterested? Do they really care if you are slouching in your chair? Will they really know if you are distracted by a quick text on your cell phone? Can they sense that you just got off a call with someone who yelled at you?

An important key to non-verbal communication is "tone". Tone comes across in everything you say on the phone. In other words, not just what you say, but how you say it. A genuine, respectful tone is what you are working for with each customer. That can be hard in claims.

You may have been told by a customer, "You're not paying me enough money!", or "You're the worst adjuster I've ever had!" or, "Connect me with your supervisor!" Those interactions can really put you in a bad mood fast. Then what happens? You pick up the phone and growl at the next customer, with your tone clearly sending a message that they don't deserve. Always remember how important your tone is for each customer.

All communication is important.

These three important factors – knowledge, empathy and communication – are your negotiating foundation. They are powerful, top priority and vital for your success. With your foundation set, your skills honed and your three step process for gaining cooperation in place, let's move on to skills specific to the settlement of a claim.

CHAPTER 9

NEGOTIATING A SETTLEMENT

**STEPS TO NEGOTIATING
A SETTLEMENT:**

1. WHY?
2. ACKNOWLEDGE
3.
4.
5. FACTS

At this point we would like to introduce a five step claims negotiation process that can be very effective when negotiating the settlement of a claim. As you can see, you already know three of the five steps.

As claims negotiators, we have a process to overcome objections that we hear on a day to day basis when we negotiate for cooperation; we ask the question, "Why?" The same question applies when negotiating for a settlement amount. Even though it's one of the most important and powerful questions we can possibly ask, we don't ask it nearly enough. A customer objects with our settlement amount and we are ready to say, "No, you're wrong" because we think we already know all the facts. Why don't we just ask the question, "Why?"

You might be saying, "Because I don't want to know the answer." Actually, we don't ask "Why?" because we're afraid of what we are going to hear or we think we might already know the answer. So, we never ask it. In this chapter, you will learn the value of this simple step in overcoming a customer's objections when negotiating the settlement amount of a claim.

Before we see how this will work with a customer, let's review the skills to remember:

- You will be listening carefully for the "thinking" and "feeling" types of statements because these are keys on how you need to respond to the customer next.
- Ask, "Why?"
- When you get their response, acknowledge it. This is a great time to show empathy. This demonstrates you heard what they said, it tells them you understand

where they are coming from, and it shows you think their answer is reasonable. You may totally disagree with their response, but that's not the important part of acknowledgement. Acknowledgement of their response to "Why?" sets the stage for the customer to listen to what you have to say on a technical level. If you discredit their response, they will not hear another word you say.

• Get back to the facts.

Let's see how claims professional, Chris, does with his customer, Mrs. Wall, when she objects to his offer:

> *Chris: "Alright Mrs. Wall. Now that we have taken the time to go over your vehicle and all of the equipment, what I'd like to do is explain to you the value of the vehicle. We have done a fair market evaluation report and we've determined the value of your vehicle is $8,000."*

> *Mrs. Wall: "$8,000! I feel my car is worth a lot more than that."*

> *Chris: "Ok, can you tell me why you feel that way?"*

Mrs. Wall: "Well, my neighbor sold a car that wasn't nearly as nice as mine and he told me he got $10,000 for his car. Not as nice as mine, I'm telling you."

Chris: "Well, your neighbor's car doesn't really have anything to do with this. I mean, do you even know what kind of car it was or the mileage it had?"

Mrs. Wall: "Does that matter?"

Chris: "Well, yes, don't you think you should know that if you're going to say your car is worth more?"

Mrs. Wall: "Well still, his car wasn't even as nice as mine. I'm not taking $8,000."

Chris: "Ok, well, you know, that's what the report says."

When Mrs. Wall objected to the settlement amount, Chris did ask, "Why." Mrs. Wall responded with her position on the claim value, using a "feeling" type statement. How did Chris do using the skills and steps above to gain Mrs. Wall's agreement with the settlement amount? Not too good.

Chris pulled out the big ole Claims Hammer, hitting Mrs. Wall over the head with the facts, telling her the reasons why her value obviously wasn't accurate. Further, Chris got distracted with conversation about the neighbor's car. Chris did ask, "Why" but then wasted the opportunity to acknowledge what the customer said with empathy before going on with the facts of the claim.

Here's another interaction between Chris and Mrs. Wall. See if you can determine what Chris can do better in his negotiation with Mrs. Wall:

> *Chris: "Alright Mrs. Wall. Now that we have taken the time to go over your vehicle and all of the equipment, what I'd like to do is explain to you the value of the vehicle. We have done a fair market evaluation report and we've determined the value of your vehicle is $8,000."*
>
> *Mrs. Wall: "$8,000! I feel my car is worth a lot more than that."*
>
> *Chris: "Can you tell me why you think $8,000 isn't fair?"*
>
> *Mrs. Wall: "Well, my neighbor sold a car that wasn't nearly as nice as mine and he told me he got $10,000 for his car. Not as nice as mine, I'm telling you."*

Chris: "Ok, we need to focus on the value of the car and the value of the car is $8,000 and that's what the report says."

Mrs. Wall: "I can't take $8,000 for the car."

Chris: "Well, that's what the value is. I mean you don't have to take it, but then we can't pay your rental anymore."

Mrs. Wall: "I can't do it."

When Chris asked, "Why?" and heard the response, he wasted no time telling Mrs. Wall why her value wasn't accurate by totally ignoring her response, blowing right past it to the facts. By not acknowledging Mrs. Wall's reason, Chris missed the opportunity to demonstrate he thought Mrs. Wall's position was reasonable, that he can understand where she was coming from. With these few words, Chris could have overcome her objection and move forward with the claims process.

Let's see Chris practice all the negotiating skills we have learned so far, demonstrating how listening and acknowledging what Mrs. Wall says is effective in separating her from the emotional tie, getting her to come over and see the facts, where Chris needs her to be:

Chris: "Alright Mrs. Wall. Now that we have taken the time to go over your vehicle and all of the equipment, what I'd like to do is explain to you the value of the vehicle. We have done a fair market evaluation report and we've determined the value of your vehicle is $8,000."

Mrs. Wall: "$8,000! I feel my car is worth a lot more than that."

Chris: "Ok, can you tell me why you feel that way?"

Mrs. Wall: "Well, my neighbor sold a car that wasn't nearly as nice as mine and he told me he got $10,000 for his car. Not as nice as mine, I'm telling you."

Chris: "Well, Mrs. Wall, if you believe your vehicle is worth more than $8,000 because your neighbor sold one for $10,000 and yours was nicer than his, I can certainly appreciate that. You know that does make sense. What I would like to do is share with you how we determined this figure because what you are entitled to is the value of the vehicle. I want to help you get what you're entitled to, so I ran this report to make sure that happens."

That was a lot better. Chris worked efficiently and effectively with Mrs. Wall to make the case; he asked, "Why?", identified the very important "feeling" of attachment to her claim value, acknowledged that her feelings around it were actually reasonable, and moved on to discuss the facts. Great negotiators don't work harder than other claims professionals; they use their skills and processes to work smarter.

So, you have three of the steps of negotiating for settlement: to ask why, to acknowledge, and get to the facts. The important thing here is for your customers to find value in the factual information that you give. To conclude the claims negotiation process we have to learn two more steps: the bridge and the agreement.

CHAPTER 10

AGREEMENT

STEPS TO NEGOTIATING
A SETTLEMENT:

1. WHY?
2. ACKNOWLEDGE
3.
4. AGREEMENT
5. FACTS

Although we still haven't discussed step# 3, we are first going to discuss step# 4 because it will help in understanding the flow of the process.

Getting "agreement" from a customer does not mean getting their agreement to actually settle for the amount of the claim that you're offering. In fact, it's to get agreement that they find value in the factual information you are giving them. In other words, it does you no good to just throw a bunch of facts at the customer if they find no value in the facts. If you can get their agreement that they will consider the facts, then you've taken great strides in your overall negotiation.

There is no better gift the customer can give you than to tell you in advance what you are about to do won't work. It will save you time and energy if you know in advance that what you are trying to do won't work. By getting the agreement step completed at this stage, you'll know if the customer finds value in your facts. If the customer is in agreement, go ahead and give them the facts. If the customer is not in agreement, you will need to take another approach.

Getting agreement is asking a "closed ended", yes or no question in one of these possible ways:

- "I would like to explain our figure, can we review it together?"
- "This report has information on your claim, can I provide it to you?"
- "You are entitled to be fully compensated, can I share with you how we determined the value?"

Your customer might think, "Sure, since you considered where I was coming from, I'll listen to you now and consider the information you have for me." If you have done a good job of asking why and really demonstrated that you consider the customer to be reasonable, they will likely agree to consider the facts you are about to give. Or they might say, "No, I'm not quite ready for that yet." Isn't it nice to know if the customer isn't ready for the facts? If the customer is not ready, you may need step# 3, which we will introduce in the next chapter.

Let's see what happens when Chris uses this new step with Mrs. Wall:

> *Chris: "Alright Mrs. Wall. Now that we have taken the time to go over your vehicle and all of the equipment, what I'd like to do is explain to you the value of the vehicle. We have done a fair market evaluation report and we've determined the value of your vehicle is $8,000."*

> *Mrs. Wall: "$8,000! I feel my car is worth a lot more than that."*

> *Chris: "Ok, can you tell me why you feel that way?"*

Mrs. Wall: "Well, my neighbor sold a car that wasn't nearly as nice as mine and he told me he got $10,000 for his car. Not as nice as mine, I'm telling you."

Chris: "Well, Mrs. Wall, if you believe your vehicle is worth more than $8,000 because your neighbor sold one for $10,000 and yours was nicer than his, I can certainly appreciate that. You know that does make sense. What I would like to do is share with you how we determined this figure because what you are entitled to is the value of the vehicle. I want to help you get what you're entitled to, so I ran this report to make sure that happens. Would you go over the report with me?"

Mrs. Wall: "I'll do that but I can't promise anything."

Chris: "Alright, that's all I ask."

Now that worked out pretty well, wouldn't you agree? When Chris asked, "Would you go over the report with me?" that was the agreement step. Let's quickly review the steps that worked to overcome the objection and get agreement to consider the facts. Chris:

- asked the question, "Why?"
- acknowledged where Mrs. Wall was coming from, demonstrating he thought she was reasonable

- got agreement from Mrs. Wall to actually look at the facts that he was about to present

That's exactly where you want to be, presenting the facts. Now, what happens when things aren't quite so easy? What happens if when you ask for an agreement, they say "No"? Do you pack it in and say, "Well, forget it then. I'm not going to settle your claim." Or do you bring out your big ole Claims Hammer and start banging away? No. You don't give up and you don't resort to other bad habits.

The important thing to remember as a claims professional is not to let customers get you flustered. Merely bring them back with "why?" It's a vital part of your process and a key to your success. It is okay to ask "why" a couple of times in a negotiation process. It very well may uncover another reason why the customer won't agree to look at the facts.

It's time for our next step. This step is crucial when things don't go quite so well during the negotiation process. It's called the Bridge.

CHAPTER 11

THE BRIDGE

**STEPS TO NEGOTIATING
A SETTLEMENT:**

1. WHY?
2. ACKNOWLEDGE
3. BRIDGE
4. AGREEMENT
5. FACTS

W e introduce the bridge last, even though it is not the last step in the process, because you don't need it every single time in the negotiation process. It's not part of the process that you'll have to use with every customer. For most customers, you will be successful going straight from why, through acknowledge, down to agreement, and then talk about the facts. You will need the bridge when you realize the circumstances are more difficult and you need that extra little push that convinces the customer to leave their feeling attachment to things and come join you in the facts.

The "bridge" is anything that you can say that gets the customer to leave behind what they believe and come join you. It makes the customer consider, "Maybe my position on this really wasn't as reasonable as I had originally thought." You can do this with solid logic, by using a hypothetical situation or an example that is opposite to their current circumstances. Without debating their reasons, the bridge simply helps the customer realize they should be open to consider other details instead of their current feelings.

This is how a bridge could work with a homeowner who has had their rug damaged. You want to replace it and you've offered $2,000. They objected to that offer. When you ask why, the customer says that they saw a personal ad for a rug like theirs and the person was asking $3,000. You acknowledge their reasoning but when you ask for agreement to review the facts, the customer says "no". That's your clue that what you are about to try won't work and you need to back up and again ask why they won't consider the $2,000. This time the customer says there is another reason, and they tell you someone offered them $3,000 once. Now you have something to work with. It's time to insert a bridge to get the customer to leave their feelings behind and come join you in the facts.

In moving the customer on in this way, you get to the point of negotiation for the settlement amount that much quicker. You are not arguing the customer's reasons; you are allowing them to self-discover they want to agree with you. The bridge is a bit trickier than the other steps of the process and knowing when and how to use it is vital to gaining agreement in more difficult negotiations.

Let's go back to Chris and Mrs. Wall and see how Chris can use a bridge to move Mrs. Wall to an agreement to discuss the facts:

> Chris: "Alright Mrs. Wall. Now that we have taken the time to go over your vehicle and all of the equipment, what I'd like to do is explain to you the value of the vehicle. We have done a fair market evaluation report and we've determined the value of your vehicle is $8,000."

> Mrs. Wall: "$8,000! I feel my car is worth a lot more than that."

> Chris: "Ok, can you tell me why you feel that way?"

Mrs. Wall: *"Well, my neighbor sold a car that wasn't nearly as nice as mine and he told me he got $10,000 for his car. Not as nice as mine, I'm telling you."*

Chris: *"Well, Mrs. Wall, if you believe your vehicle is worth more than $8,000 because your neighbor sold one for $10,000 and yours was nicer than his, I can certainly appreciate that. You know that does make sense. What I would like to do is share with you how we determined this figure because what you are entitled to is the value of the vehicle. I want to help you get what you're entitled to, so I ran this report to make sure that happens. Would you go over the report with me?"*

Mrs. Wall: *"No."*

Chris: *"Can you tell me why you wouldn't want to look at the figures?"*

Mrs. Wall: *"Well, to be honest with you, I owe $9,000 on this car."*

Chris: *"So you owe more than $8,000, you actually owe $9,000, is that what you're saying?"*

Mrs. Wall: *"That's correct."*

Chris: *"And that's why you believe it's worth more than $8,000?"*

Mrs. Wall: "Correct."

Chris: "If that's why, it is very reasonable. I certainly understand that and can appreciate your position. Let me ask you this, Mrs. Wall. If you only owed $4,000 on your car, and that's all you had left to pay, you wouldn't want us to just pay you $4,000, am I right?"

Mrs. Wall: "Yeah, that's right."

Chris: "As you can see, what you owe on the car isn't really an indicator of its value. What you're entitled to under the policy is the value of your vehicle, and again, in order to make sure you get what you're entitled to, I ran this report. Now you don't have to agree with the figures, but I would at least like to be able to show these to you so you can understand where we got these figures. Would that be alright?"

Mrs. Wall: "Sure, but I really can't promise anything."

Chris: "Alright, that's good enough."

Chris used his process to negotiate this claim, and when he got an objection from the customer to move on to look at his factual information, he knew there was something more going on. Chris went right back to "why" again and got to the bottom of Mrs. Wall's reasons for not cooperating. He acknowledged her reasons and knew, at that point, he would need to give Mrs. Wall a solid reason why she should leave behind her feelings and come join him in the facts. That solid reason was the "bridge" and it convinced Mrs. Wall to agree to leave her feelings behind and hear the facts, putting Chris one step closer to being able to negotiate for the settlement amount.

The bridge is used when customers are not cooperating because they are tied to their feelings. Sometimes those feelings are very personal and the customer can be very passionate about the situation. Our customers have every right to their feelings. To demonstrate, take a look at this interaction between claims adjuster, Beth, and homeowner, Albert, whose computer has been stolen:

> *Beth: "Albert, I see here by the documentation we have, that your computer is worth $1,500 and we can go ahead and pay you that now."*

> *Albert: "No way, Beth, absolutely no way! I want at least $5,000!"*

> *Beth: "Why $5,000, Albert? It's only worth $1,500."*

Albert: "I'll tell you why, because I was working on my MBA, and I've got two years of research papers, I've got two years of homework assignments, I've got two years of my life tied up in this computer. Man, $1,500 is a total joke!"

Beth: "Well, Albert, I can see here from the documentation that the computer is only worth $1,500. I can show you the documentation, I mean, it says right here, it's replaceable for $1,500. Can I show you this?"

Albert: "No, Beth, I told you, I have my life tied up in this thing and $1,500 is not going to do it."

Beth: "Well, that's all we have. That's all I can pay you."

Albert: "Beth, I'm not going to take it."

What's the main problem with this conversation? Beth and Albert are actually talking about two different things. Beth is talking about the value of the computer and Albert is talking about the computer with the data – data that is very important to him emotionally. Beth hasn't explained to Albert that the policy covers the value of the computer, not the data. When Beth explains, she will need to get Albert's "agreement" that he understands what he is (and what he isn't) being paid for. Until Beth does her job and gets Albert's agreement that he's not going to get paid for the data, they are quite literally talking about two different things. What a waste of time and energy for both Beth and Albert, who is already distraught.

A bridge can just be telling the customer what is covered. Let's see how Beth does with Albert when she uses the process.

> *Beth: "Albert, I see here by the documentation we have that your computer is worth $1,500 and we can go ahead and pay you that now."*
>
> *Albert: "No way, Beth, absolutely no way! I want at least $5,000!"*
>
> *Beth: "Why $5,000, Albert?"*
>
> *Albert: "I'll tell you why, because I was working on my MBA, and I've got two years of research papers, I've got two years of homework assignments, I've got two years of my life tied up in this computer. Man, $1,500 is a total joke!"*
>
> *Beth: "Albert, I can appreciate all the hard work you have put into your MBA. It sounds like the computer is a tremendous loss and I'm sorry that happened to you. If I could pay you for the hard work and all the material you lost, I surely would. Albert, your policy does have limitations on what we can and can't pay for. Your policy covers only the computer, not the data."*

Albert: "Wow, it sounds like your saying I'm not going to get paid for all the data? I'm only getting paid for the computer?"

Beth: "Correct. I would love to be able to pay you for the data but can't. What I can pay you for is the computer itself, and based on the information at hand, the documentation says I can pay you $1,500. If you agree, I can pay you the $1,500 now and help you put this theft behind you."

Albert: "Fine."

Beth listened and heard how important that computer was to her customer. She didn't argue with Albert or make him feel his work wasn't important. Even though she had to deliver bad news, Beth used the process to help Albert understand what was being paid and why. Even though Albert was emotional, Beth used a bridge to bring him over to discuss the facts; she moved effectively and efficiently through why, acknowledge, bridge, agreement and facts.

Now you have all the steps for negotiation: ask "why", acknowledge the reasons, use a bridge when you need it, get agreement to look at the facts, and then discuss the facts themselves. Consider the following scenario to practice the steps of the process:

> You are handling an injury claim; could be a worker's comp claim, a slip and fall, or it could be an auto accident. You've offered $10,000 to settle their injury. The customer responds they feel their claim is worth at least $15,000. You respond:

> a) You are mistaken. Your claim is only worth $10,000.
> b) Better take what you can get.
> c) Can I ask why you think your claim is worth more than $10,000?

> The customer responds because they read an article in the paper where a lady got $1.4 million just for spilling coffee on her leg, so their claim must get them at least $15,000. You respond with this acknowledgement statement:

> a) This has nothing to do with coffee.
> b) I don't think you heard me. The offer is $10,000.
> c) I can appreciate if you saw an article where someone got $1.4M for spilling coffee on their leg.

I understand why you might feel your claim is worth more.

If the customer won't move on to discuss the facts, what bridge might you use to get them to leave their emotional or feeling attachment behind and start talking about the facts surrounding the case:

a) Reading the newspaper is just confusing you.
b) That lady is lucky she got what she did.
c) My guess is that neither one of us knows all the facts surrounding that case. Would you agree we need to focus on your claim and your injuries?

When the customer is ready to move on, which statement might you use to gain their agreement to discuss the facts?

a) I'm ready to get your claim finished, aren't you?
b) I'm exhausted so I can only imagine how you feel. Ready to wrap it up?
c) If we can talk about what you went through, your injuries and your medical bills, I'm sure we can help you get this claim resolved and get this all behind you. Can we do that now?

Another technique used by great claims negotiators is the "opening statement". Let's learn how to use this to make your job easier and to deliver world class service. Are you ready?

CHAPTER 12

THE OPENING STATEMENT

In a trial, lawyers make an opening statement that can set the stage for the entire proceeding. During their opening statement, the judge, jury and observers are all keenly focused on the attorneys, hanging on their every word. In claims, you have this same opportunity to make an opening statement with your customer. This is the time when you present your information; when you lay out your facts to the customer.

Think of an opening statement as making a great first impression. This can set the stage for your entire negotiation. Great claims negotiators always include a well thought out opening statement. Doing this is valuable, and takes effort and practice.

Consider the following face-to-face negotiation between claims adjuster, Terry, and his customer, Mr. Glenn. This will give you a chance to evaluate what Terry does and doesn't do well in his opening statement:

Terry: "Hello, Mr. Glenn, I'm Terry."

Mr. Glenn: "Oh, hi Terry, thanks for finally showing up."

Terry: "Yeah, I'm a little late, your directions weren't too good. Tell you what, do you have a place we could sit down and go over this?"

Mr. Glenn: "Sure, right over here at the table."

Terry: "This table works great. You go and take that seat across from me – that's good. What I'd like to do is see if I can't get rid of this thing, pay you something for your injuries, and we'll put this behind us. Now, here's what I've got – let's cover this quick. I have that you had about $5,000 in meds and about $1,000 loss of earnings. You took off an entire week for your injuries – wow - I'm going to let that slide. Tell you what I'll do, since this isn't that serious, I'm going to go ahead and pay $10,000, see if we can't get rid of this thing because really, it's gone on long enough. Alright, so how does $10,000 sound to you?"

Mr. Glenn: "Well, that can't include my pain and suffering because I was expecting a lot more."

Terry: "Suffering? Really, suffering? Mr. Glenn that amount does include your pain and suffering. $10,000 is a lot of money. How does that sound?"

Mr. Glenn: "It doesn't sound good at all."

Terry: "Ah, okay, well how much were you hoping for?"

Mr. Glenn: "I was looking for at least $30,000."

Terry: "What?! $30,000! How did you come up with that, Mr. Glenn?"

Mr. Glenn: "Well, my next door neighbor, he had the same accident, his car was totaled just like mine and he got $30,000 for his pain."

Terry: "Look, we're not here to talk about your neighbor. We're here to talk about you. And your case is worth $10,000 at the most. Like I said, this isn't that serious, it's not like your leg was cut off, know what I mean? Tell you what, here's what I'll do to speed this along. I'll go ahead and throw in an extra $1,000, make it $11,000, just to make this thing go away. Does that sound good?"

Mr. Glenn: "The $11,000 isn't going to make it go away for me, Terry. I mean, I missed a softball game, plus I couldn't go bowling with my wife."

Terry: "You mentioned missing the softball game before, so I already had that. I found out your team is in last place so I don't think the world is going to end because you missed a game. That's not a good reason

I should pay you more than $11,000. Give me another reason to pay you more."

Mr. Glenn: "I should be paid more because I missed a week's worth of work and that was $1,000. I don't think you considered that."

Terry: "Come on, Mr. Glenn! Most people don't make $1,000 sitting around watching The Today Show! You are going to have to come down from $30,000 because I'm too smart to bid against myself. So, unless you come down from $30,000, there's nothing I can do."

Mr. Glenn: "I'll come down as much as you went up. I want $29,000."

Terry: "Really, I was hoping you were going to be reasonable about this. I mean, $30,000, $29,000, that's out of control. I've told you why your case is only worth $11,000 and you haven't given me any good reason why your case is worth $29,000."

Mr. Glenn: "Well, because, like I told you, my neighbor got about the same injury and damages as I did with my accident."

Terry: "Rather than talk about your neighbor again, here's what we'll do. I'll go ahead and bump it up one last time to $11,500 just to get rid of this thing. I've actually got other appointments this afternoon. If you *can't take my last offer... then you can't take it. Just remember, you're the one that has to pay your bills and stuff. So, I'll leave the $11,500 offer on the table. Why don't you talk about it with your wife and let me know."*

Mr. Glenn: "Alright, fine."

Terry: "Great. I've got to run."

We have Terry performing poorly in this interaction to give you a lot to learn from. Let's get started evaluating how Terry did in his "opening statement" with Mr. Glenn:

ACTION	ISSUE
Terry was late to the appointment	Instead of apologizing, Terry blamed Mr. Glenn, insulting him by saying his directions weren't good. That is not going to go over too well when trying to negotiate a case.
Terry told Mr. Glenn to sit across the table from him	Two errors here. First, respect that it's Mr. Glenn's house. Ask, instead of tell, where the customer is comfortable sitting. Second, Terry sitting across the table from Mr. Glenn puts a barrier between them. Terry being on one side and Mr. Glenn on the other feels like there is going to be a fight and someone is going to win. If you negotiate in person, never sit directly across from the

	customer. Move your chair in a more neutral position. You will gain the most credibility by sitting side-by-side with the customer, where they can see what you are looking at.
Terry's pace of conversation	Terry wanted to get through the discussion with Mr. Glenn quickly. When you're speaking to a customer, respect how important this is to them and slow down. The normal rate of speech is about 125 words per minute. To slow down from that might be uncomfortable to you but the customer needs to really register this information.
Terry insisted on getting an amount from Mr. Glenn	You are the expert, not the customer. Keep the customer in your conversation. When Terry asked, "How much were you hoping for?", he sent Mr. Glenn away to his conversation, which implies what Mr. Glenn thinks actually has an impact on the value of the claim. Some claims people believe it's a good technique to ask the customer what they want so you know where they are. Most great negotiators say that is not a good technique. Great negotiators say by asking how much he was hoping for, Terry put himself on equal ground with Mr. Glenn and lends credibility to the

	amount Mr. Glenn thinks he should receive. Mr. Glenn isn't the expert, Terry is. Terry knows the value, has the research, he has the training, he has the experience. Keep the customer in your conversation by asking why what you're offering is not enough, rather than asking how much they want.
Terry discounted all of Mr. Glenn's reasons	Customers want to be understood, to feel you are listening to them; they need to know you appreciate their point of view. Terry asked Mr. Glenn why, then argued every one of his reasons and completely discounted the value of his activities.
Terry asked Mr. Glenn to be reasonable	Terry sent the message that Mr. Glenn is an unreasonable person. If you want your customer to be reasonable, the worst thing you can do is tell them they have to be reasonable. If you want your customer to be reasonable, show them you already think they are.
Terry blamed Mr. Glenn for the claim dragging on	Terry told Mr. Glenn his claim had gone on long enough, which made Mr. Glenn feel it was his fault and put him on the defensive. Mr. Glenn was injured and Terry expressed no empathy, even minimized all the impacts of the accident.

Terry is in a hurry to get to other appointments	There is nothing more important than the customer you are dealing with right now. Terry telling Mr. Glenn he has other appointments made it seem other things were more important than Mr. Glenn.

There are certainly a lot of lessons to learn from Terry's "opening statement" with Mr. Glenn. Terry is going to try again and we want you to consider all the improvements in his opening statement and interaction with Mr. Glenn:

Terry: "Mr. Glenn?"

Mr. Glenn: "Yes, are you Terry?"

Terry: "Yes, I am. How are you doing?"

Mr. Glenn: "Great, thanks for finally showing up."

Terry: "I know I'm a little late and certainly apologize for that. I understand this is important. I hope I haven't kept you waiting too long."

Mr. Glenn: "Not too long, at all."

Terry: "Ok, great. Thanks so much for your time. Do you have a place we can sit down and chat?"

Mr. Glenn: "Yeah, come on in. Why don't you have a seat right here?"

Terry: "You know, I've got a lot of information to show you, I'm going to slide on over here if you don't mind so we can look at the information together. Is that alright?"

Mr. Glenn: "That's fine."

Terry: "Well, before we get started, I want to find out how you are feeling."

Mr. Glenn: "You know, a little sore still but I feel much better."

Terry: "Oh, that's good to hear. I read the doctor's report and he said you are still going to have some residual pain but basically you're on your way to healing and that's good. I am sorry something like this even had to happen to you. So you know, I want to tell you that my main goal is to make sure that we fairly compensate you for your injuries. That's my main goal. What I'd like to do before we talk about money is to explain to you how we evaluate a case like yours. I believe you are entitled to that. Would that be alright?"

Mr. Glenn: "Yeah, that'd be great, I appreciate that."

Terry: "Okay, the very first thing that we do is gather all the medical records. That's the doctor's visit, the chiropractor visit and even the emergency vehicle. All of that came to $4,399.74. Does that sound about right to you?"

Mr. Glenn: "Yeah, I think that's the same number I came up with."

Terry: "Alright, the next thing that we do is gather your lost wages. You were nice enough to sign that medical authorization and the wage release so we got the information from your employer. They said you missed five days at $200 a day so basically that's $1,000. They did tell us that you were paid for those days because you took sick days. Nevertheless, it's still fair that you get compensated for that because you wouldn't have had to take those sick days if you didn't have the accident. So, it's only fair to go ahead and include the $1,000 in our evaluation. Does that sound fair?"

Mr. Glenn: "Yeah, it does."

Terry: "Okay, great. The next thing we do is look for any other expenses that might be related to the actual injury that have a specific dollar amount. Is there anything that I missed as far as the medical bills and your lost wages or anything else?"

Mr. Glenn: "Yes, because my car was in the shop, I had to take a cab to the doctor's office a couple of times. That was, I think $75.00 it came up to."

Terry: "$75.00 total?"

Mr. Glenn: "Correct, for both trips."

Terry: "Mr. Glenn, let me make a note of that since I didn't know that before. I have it now. Well, the next thing we do is determine the value of the case and that has to include what's called general damages. You might have heard the term "pain and suffering" before. What that really means is inconvenience. You mentioned that because of the accident, you missed playing some softball games, which I know was difficult for you, and that you missed your son's wedding and I understand that was very difficult. Was there anything else that occurred that, you know, we should have considered as part of this?"

Mr. Glenn: "No, other than, like you said, the general inconvenience of having my back hurt."

Terry: "Alright, for each case we gather all the information and come to an evaluation. Before I tell you what that is, I did have one notation down here that the adjuster who had the case before me said there was a problem at the body shop. Something about they had run out of parts or something, and he had to extend the rental car five extra days so you wouldn't be inconvenienced. Was that helpful for you?"

Mr. Glenn: "Oh, yes, the extension was great and really got me out of a bind at the time."

Terry: "Okay, so that issue is over. Can I cross that off our file?"

Mr. Glenn: "Sure."

Terry: "Well, it sounds like we have everything. With that, we are ready to evaluate your case. Even though we use our experiences with similar cases, similar injuries, and see what other cases have settled for, we look at your case individually. It does take a certain amount of investigation and a certain amount of experience to evaluate injury cases. We have evaluated the information of your case and I have full authority to settle your case today. Normally a case like this would go anywhere from $9,000 to $9,500, you know, I've even seen them go up to $10,000 before. What I want to be able to do is pay you the $10,000, add in that $75.00 that we talked about and make the entire settlement package $10,075. With this, hopefully you will feel completely compensated and if I can pay you $10,075 today, you can start to put this behind you. How does that sound?"

Mr. Glenn: "Well, I was looking for $25,000."

Terry: "Okay, what is it about $10,075 that doesn't sound good to you?"

Terry can now start the negotiation process. If you listed all the things that Terry did well in this negotiation "opening statement", you have a long list. Let's take a quick review:

Terry was late to the appointment	Terry made no excuses. He apologized and told Mr. Glenn he knew the appointment was important and he thanked Mr. Glenn for his time. We are in the customer service business and these quick statements earn Terry credibility for valuing the customer and prepare the customer to move on to business.
Terry asked where they could sit	Terry explained he had materials to share with Mr. Glenn and asked if they could sit side-by-side. Terry would have brought only the materials he needed to share from the file.
Terry focused on empathy and fairness	Terry asked Mr. Glenn how he was feeling, stated how good it was he was healing, and said he was sorry that it even happened. Apologizing to

	the customer sounds to them like the responsible party apologizing. That can go a long way. Terry also stated his goal to be fair in the compensation and how he determined the evaluation. Finally, Terry told Mr. Glenn he was entitled to these things and asked Mr. Glenn if it was alright to proceed with the explanation. These are strong, positive negotiation techniques. It lets the person know, you understand that their time is valuable. But it also lets them know you're willing to take the time to go over this because they are entitled to that information. That's a very powerful tool.
Terry explained the leg work of the case	Without boring the customer with every single detail, Terry let Mr. Glenn know he had taken the time and effort to find all the information, that he had done his homework. That's a great technique.
Terry complimented Mr. Glenn	Even if it's minor, small expressions of appreciation go a long way with our customers. They may even work hard to earn your acknowledgement. Terry told Mr. Glenn he was nice enough to sign the medical authorization and loss of earnings form. Just saying a customer is nice to do something, can translate as you think they are a nice

	person and they will try to meet that. Plan this technique ahead and state your appreciation for something they have done for you during the process.
Terry pointed out concessions	This technique also requires planning in advance to make sure you aren't bringing up a bad circumstance, that the customer actually views the concessions as fair and positive to them. Terry reminded Mr. Glenn that the rental had been extended, and he also stated the loss of earnings wouldn't be impacted by paid sick days he had taken. These were both positive concessions that demonstrate to Mr. Glenn that Terry is on his side and working hard to be fair.
Terry asked for any additional information he didn't already have	After explaining all the details he knew, Terry asked Mr. Glenn if there was anything else, and if there were any additional general damages. This shows the customer you are listening and gets all the cards on the table before discussing the dollar amount. Terry didn't pretend he already knew about the $75 for the taxi, and then gained credibility by bringing the $75 specifically into the total settlement.

Terry explained in common terms	Terry explained terms to soften them up and bring them down to a less punitive impact on Mr. Glenn. He turned "Pain and Suffering" to "Inconvenience".
Terry mentioned experience needed	Why would Terry tell Mr. Glenn it takes investigation and experience to evaluate a case? Because it does, the customer doesn't have it. You can make the statement without making the customer feel stupid. This is another way to keep them in your conversation, and not to go down to their level by asking the customer what they think their claim is worth.
Terry planted a seed on what was to come	Terry told Mr. Glenn he had seen cases like his go from $9,000 to $9,500, even go up to $10,000 before. When Terry made the offer, he said the case is "worth up to" and we can pay Mr. Glenn the "entire" $10,000. Terry did not say the word "only" during the conversation. This is a powerful technique. Practice using it when you can and when appropriate.

Terry used his process	Terry made the offer and asked Mr. Glenn how it sounded. Mr. Glenn told Terry the amount he expected. Terry kept Mr. Glenn in his conversation, asking why the $10,075 didn't sound good. The opening statement set the stage for the negotiation.

In chapter 1, we told you that great negotiators have a process and you have read several interactions putting the process to work. The process is supported by an effective and well thought out "opening statement". The "opening statement" looks a little complicated and might feel lengthy as you get familiar with it but you can do this. Keep a list of special phrases handy to use with your customers, express genuine empathy, study your case for concessions, remove the word "only" from your vocabulary, compliment your customer and always remember, you are in the customer service business.

In the next chapter, we give you more power tools.

CHAPTER 13

POWERFUL CONCEPTS AND TECHNIQUES

W hether you are settling a worker's comp claim, a bodily injury, a total loss automobile claim or a construction defect, great claims negotiators tell us the following techniques and concepts are powerful tools in the claims negotiating process.

Delivering Bad News

As a claims professional, you often have to deliver bad news. You have to say "No" for so many different reasons: from there is no liability, to there is no coverage, to you can't pay more than the liability limits, to you can't waive the deductible, and more. Don't shy away from delivering bad news. You are in the customer service business and even delivering bad news is an opportunity to have an impact on the customer. It's all in how you deliver the message and you are in control. As a professional, this is when you plan ahead and prepare your message.

Delivering bad news is the perfect time to express empathy with a short and clear empathic statement. This demonstrates you are a human being and you understand the customer is, too. Who knows, a little bit of empathy, and you might even get a "Thank You" at the end of the conversation.

In chapter 4, we learned when repeating reasons back to the customer during the acknowledgement step, never say "but" and debate the reason. We learned to remove the "but". When delivering bad news, take extra care to say "and" not "but" in the sentence. Saying "but" removes the positive impact from the front of the sentence and shifts the focus on the negative. "Leading with the positive" still delivers the necessary bad news to the customer and helps the customer see you are working to help them.

Just like when you are on the receiving end of bad news, the customer has a right to how they feel. During the negotiation process, the customer may respond when you deliver the news. Don't consider this as an attack on you or a reason to argue. Listen carefully to the customer and take this as a gift. An example is you tell the customer you can't pay for part or their entire claim and they respond, "Oh, that's lousy" or "that really stinks." There's your gift. That response tells you, even though they don't like the news, they do believe you and understand what you just said. Here is where you can express empathy again, which will help mend the wound.

Great negotiators use their skill in delivering bad news to their customers and keep the negotiation moving along to closure.

Staying in Your Conversation

Often times, you will need to ask customers, "Why do you feel the way you feel?" You want to discover that information from the customer and you don't want to do it in a way that sends them off into outer space with completely unreasonable expectations. The idea of "staying in your conversation" keeps the customer in reality. Your success in doing that hinges on how you ask the question.

A valuable concept for any claims person is to appreciate the more time you spend talking about your information, your facts, and why your figures are correct, the more likely it will settle closer to your figure. The more time you spend talking about the other person's information, their facts, and why their figures are correct, the more likely it will settle closer to their figure. This leads us to our Claims Maxim #5.

Maxim #5: Claims negotiation is matter of time. (See Figure 13.1)

Usually we hear adjusters asking the right question, but in the wrong way. Grace is trying to settle a commercial slip and fall accident with the claimant, Albert. Here is how we often here the conversation go:

> Grace: "Albert, we have evaluated your case. We've looked at the medical records. We've looked at the bills. We've looked at everything you and I have spoken about as far as the value of this case and we've put a value of $5,000 on this case. We want to pay you $5,000 today. How does that sound?"
>
> Albert: "Well, I have to tell you, Grace, I really believe that my claim is worth at least $50,000."
>
> Grace: "Albert, can you tell me why you believe it is worth $50,000?"

Albert: "Yeah, I'll tell you why. I mean, I missed some time from work. I had some medical bills. You know, it was pretty traumatic for my kids, and of course, you know, not being able to play the piano and missing those croquet lessons was really important to me. I think $50,000 seems fair."

Grace: "Albert, $50,000 is just too much. I'm sure it wasn't "traumatic" for your kids. Kids accept things pretty well. As far as being off of work, we're paying you for that, and you don't even have to pay tax on it. And how do we know you ever could play the piano? And croquet lessons? I'm sure you can pick up where you left off."

Albert: "Fine. How about $45,000 then?"

Did you notice that because Grace asked Albert why he wanted $50,000, the entire conversation is going to center around that figure? More importantly, every word that comes out of Albert's mouth is convincing him more and more that $50,000 is correct. And worse, now that Grace has allowed Albert to talk in terms of $50,000, she has to try to prove him wrong to get him to come down.

However, remember, you never have to prove anyone wrong. But in this case, that is exactly what Grace is going to have to do because she in not in her conversation. You see, the question isn't, "Why do you want $50,000?" The question should be, "Why isn't $5,000 enough?"

It may seem like semantics, but it is not. If Grace asks the question the right way, she can acknowledge what Albert says in order to prove herself right instead of having to prove Albert wrong.

Let's see how it works with this time with Grace asking the right question:

> Grace: *"Albert, we have evaluated your case. We've looked at the medical records. We've looked at the bills, and your lost wages of $800.00. We've looked at everything you and I have spoken about as far as the value of this case and we've put a value of $5,000 on this case. We want to pay you $5,000 today. How does that sound?"*
>
> Albert: *"Well, I have to tell you, Grace, I really believe that my claim is worth at least $50,000."*
>
> Grace: *"Albert, can you tell me why you believe it is worth more than $5,000? Why doesn't $5,000 seem fair?"*

Albert: "It's got to be worth more than $5,000! I mean, I missed some time from work. I had some medical bills. You know, it was pretty traumatic for my kids, and of course, you know, not being able to play the piano and missing those croquet lessons was really important to me."

Grace: "Well, I do appreciate what you just said. I am glad we are including $800.00 your lost time from work in that figure. And I do recognize that you experienced personal inconvenience such as not playing the piano and your croquet lessons. You know those are all things that we talked about before. As a matter of fact, Albert, those were all factors that went into the $5,000. So $5,000 does seem to be accurate."

Albert: "No $5,000 is not going to cut it. You know, I'd like more than $5,000."

Grace: "Okay, Albert, we're not finished quite yet. I can alter the evaluation to be extra fair."

Did you see what happened in this conversation? Grace was able to get Albert to stop talking about why he wants $50,000 and start talking about why he wants more than $5,000. That's exactly where Grace wants Albert. It is okay that Albert wants more than $5,000. Grace has more than $5,000. What she doesn't have is $50,000 or even close to that.

In one conversation, Grace changes Albert's focus and that is a very powerful skill. Grace was able to get Albert into her conversation. Will it work 100% of the time? No, nothing does. But it works a lot. And you are always better discussion the settlement in terns of your figure instead of their figure.

Figure 13.1

Carl Van's Claims Negotiation Maxims

The most important thing to remember when negotiating the settlement of any claim is that we are in the customer service business. We are in the business of helping people. Even if someone does not get everything they want, as long as they still feel they were treated with respect by a knowledgeable professional, who cares about doing a good job, they may just be satisfied.

Claims Maxim #1: **People will consider your point of view to the exact degree you have demonstrated you understand their point of view.** (Listen! Then paraphrase back what you hear)

Claims Maxim #2:   **Great claims negotiators never argue with reasons, they argue the facts.** (Acknowledge their reasons and move on)

Claims Maxim #3:   **You never have to prove anyone wrong, you only have to prove yourself right.** (No one likes to be wrong, so don't waste your time)

Claims Maxim #4:   **People trust someone who is trying to help them and don't trust someone who is trying to hurt them.** (Put away the Claims Hammer for a moment)

Claims Maxim #5:   **Claims negotiation is a matter of time.** (Stay in your conversation)

In this case, Albert has his reasons. Did you notice what Grace was able to do with those reasons? She was able to use all of Albert's reasons to reinforce she was on track with the $5,000. What Grace doesn't want to do is argue with Albert, to point out why he is wrong with each point he brings up. Great negotiators never argue with reasons. They acknowledge the reasons and use them to demonstrate to the customer that they are right. Never spend your time and effort convincing the customer they are wrong. Use your skills to convince the customer you are right!

Bidding Against Yourself

We've all heard the phrase "never bid against yourself". For the most part, that is an accurate practice. There is an exception. Great claims negotiators know you can bid against yourself, as long as you stay in your conversation. "Staying in your conversation" means you talk about $5,000 and increase it to $5,500 and increase it to $5,750, rather than waste your time trying to bring the customer down from $50,000.

You can bid against yourself all day as long as you and the customer stay in your conversation. Your conversation is your value of the claim, and that's where you want to be.

Bidding against your initial offer is okay when it influences the customer, as in the case of Albert and Grace. The trick is to stay in your conversation.

When to Increase Your Offer

Just like with humor, timing is everything. During the negotiation, many claims professionals will increase their offer when the other side has made a good point. We hear this all the time while monitoring claims phone calls. The customer or other party makes a good point and the next thing said is, "Okay, let me increase the offer" or the dreaded, "Let me throw in a little bit of money." This is the wrong time to increase the offer.

This practice conditions the customer that every time they make a good point; you are going to reward them with more money. Think about a pet you trained by giving them a treat to reinforce behavior you wanted them to continue. If you "reward" the customer with an increased offer when they make a point, what are you training them to do? Make more points.

The best time to increase your offer is once you've demonstrated to the customer that you shouldn't *have* to increase your offer. The powerful concept here is to demonstrate to the customer that your offer is already fair, and then you can increase it.

You can see how this concept worked for Grace in her negotiation with Albert. Grace made the offer of $5,000 and Albert said, no way, he believed his claim was worth at least $50,000. Grace asked why, and gave Albert the opportunity to state all his reasons. Grace didn't "reward" him immediately by increasing the offer, making him think he "won" and can continue making points. She acknowledged Albert's point of view, expressed empathy for the situation, and "made her case" that those are the exact reasons for the $5,000 offer, which seems to be accurate and fair. Grace knows she can go over the $5,000 but doesn't alter the evaluation until the timing is right. The timing is best when you demonstrate you really shouldn't have to increase the offer.

Great claims negotiators know this timing is powerful because it makes the customer feel you have made a concession and are being *extra* fair. When making the increased offer, it is important you make it sound like a concession for you, instead of a "win" for the customer. A "win" for the customer would tempt some customers to continue pushing for increases. Just remember, timing is everything.

In chapter 14, you will get a snapshot of the top four behaviors that you want with all your customers and ways to promote those behaviors.

CHAPTER 14

EXCEL WITH YOUR CUSTOMERS

As we learned in earlier chapters, many times in claims, you are negotiating simply for a response from a customer. In this chapter, we will provide four examples of things we hear often while monitoring phone calls, which can have the opposite effect from what is intended. We will look at the pitfalls with certain words and propose options to help you say it best and excel with your customers.

<u>Trying to get a customer to be patient:</u>

> The adjuster says, *"Sir, you're going to have to be patient."*

> The customer hears, *"Sir, since I'm not taking your situation seriously, and I'm overworked, and don't*

really have the time necessary to do a good job for you, you're going to have to be patient."

The adjuster should say, *"Sir, I understand the need to get this claim resolved promptly and efficiently for you. I will do everything I can to keep it moving."*

Trying to get a customer to trust you:

The adjuster says, "Sir, *you are going to have to trust me on this."*

The customer hears, *"Sir, I have no reason for the things I do or say. If I did, I would explain them to you in a way you could understand. So, question everything I tell you. And for heaven's sake, DON'T TRUST ME."*

The adjuster should say, *"Sir, you have every right to question the process. You, like me, want to make sure you get everything you are entitled to. I'll do my best to make things clear."*

Trying to get a customer to calm down:

The adjuster says, *"Sir, I don't know if there is any reason to get excited over this."*

The customer hears, *"Sir, you have no reason for your actions, and your feelings have no value. What a hysterical moron you are."*

The adjuster should say, *"Sir, I can understand why you are frustrated. Let me see if I can help."*

Trying to get a customer to be reasonable:

> The adjuster says, *"Sir, you are going to have to be reasonable about this."*

> The customer hears, *"Sir, you are not a reasonable person. I'm going to make you change your mind. And when you do, you'll be proving that I was right for calling you unreasonable."*

> The adjuster should say, *"Sir, I understand your points. You are obviously a reasonable person. You are entitled to an explanation, and I'd like to provide that to you now."*

You are in control of your own behavior and how you speak to your customers. On the flip side, your customers have a right to how they feel. So, whether it's asking a customer to be reasonable, to be patient, to trust you more or to calm down, say it the best way to show respect and move the claims process forward.

CHAPTER 15

WORDS TO AVOID

There are words that we use freely that are a normal part of our terminology, but are best not used when discussing settlement with a customer. We would like to at least pose some alternatives for you to use as part of your everyday discussions with customers.

Most of these terms are fine to use with attorneys, but with unrepresented customers, you may want to avoid them.

Offer

We use the word "offer" so much that it is hard to imagine not using it when we discuss the value of a claim. But think about what the word "offer" really means. It pretty much means, "This is not what I think the claim is worth, this is just my 'offer'." When you use the word "offer", you have just planted a seed in the person's mind that there is more to come.

> Don't say, *"We want to offer you $5,000 for your claim."*
>
> Say, *"Your claim has been evaluated at $5,000, and we want to pay you that full amount"*

About

When you use the word "about" while describing the damages, you sound as if you are not certain. Use exact terms.

> Don't say, *"Your bills are about $2,000.00."*
>
> Say, *"Your bills come to $2,023.19."*

Willing to

When you use the words "willing to" you sound as if you are only doing what is right because you have to, but you would rather not. In a way, you are admitting you would get out of paying the claim if you could.

> Don't say, *"We are willing to pay you $10,000."*
>
> Say, *"We want to pay you what you are entitled to, which is $10,000."*

Only

When you use the word "only", you are making the customer think that you devalue their case, and whatever figure you use, will not be enough.

Don't say, *"We can only pay you $8,000."*

Say, *"Your claim is worth up to $8,000."*

Throw in

When you use the words "throw in", "bump up", or similar sounding phrases when increasing your offer, it gives the customer the impression that more money is easy to get.

Don't say, *"Let me throw in another $500."*

Say, *"I am going to alter the evaluation by $500."*

Don't owe

When you use the words "don't owe", you make it sound like we won and they lost.

Don't say, *"We don't owe you anything for that. It's not covered."*

Say, *"I want to make sure you get everything you are entitled to. Let me explain what is covered."*

Or

Say, *"If there was a way we could pay you for that, I would love to do it. The policy restricts what we can and cannot pay for. Can we review it together?"*

Great claims professionals know the optimal use of their time and effort is in preparation for the negotiation. In the next few chapters, you learn the skills that will help you prepare winning conversations.

CHAPTER 16

NEGOTIATING WITH ATTORNEYS

Staying in Your Conversation (revisited)

Back in chapter 13 we discussed the power of staying in your conversation. Remember Maxim #5? **Negotiation is a matter of time.** This is also very true when negotiating with attorneys.

In claims, we are on the losing end of this concept most of the time. In monitoring phone calls, we can tell you that at least 80% of the time, the conversation centers around the attorney's demand instead of the adjuster's evaluation.

Here is a typical conversation between attorney Mark Steely and the adjuster Dan:

> *Dan: "Mr. Steely, this in Dan from Typical Insurance Company. I'm calling to discuss settlement of your Client Mr. Dupree"*
>
> *Mr. Steely: "Yes, that's great. Did you get my demand package for $100,000?"*
>
> *Dan: "Yes, I got it. But there is no way this is worth $100,000."*
>
> *Mr. Steely: "Why not? Give me one reason."*
>
> *Dan: "I'll give you several..."*

At this point, Dan is going to launch into all of the reasons why the claim is not worth $100,000. They will go back and forth, and Mr. Steely might come down a little. And after 45 minutes, when all the bickering is done, maybe, just maybe, Dan will throw out his $20,000 offer. By the time they have finished talking about $100,000 for 45 minutes, that $20,000 is going to seem like a paltry figure, even to Dan.

The point is, even with attorneys, negotiation is a matter of time. Our suggestion is to stop talking about demands, and start talking abut the value of the claim. Why waste 45 minutes talking about a figure you know the attorney just made up anyway? You have spent a lot of time reviewing the case, evaluating the information and doing your research. Talk about your figure, not theirs.

Let's give Dan another try after teaching him the value of staying in his conversation:

> Dan: "Mr. Steely, this in Dan from Typical Insurance Company. I'm calling to discuss settlement of your Client Mr. Dupree"
>
> Mr. Steely: "Yes, that's great. Did you get my demand package for $100,000?"
>
> Dan: "Yes, I got it. But I'd really rather talk about the value of the claim. Based on all of the information you provided, the total of the damages, along with our theory of comparative liability on the part of your client, we have evaluated this case at $20,000, and I would like to extend that full amount to your client now."
>
> Mr. Steely: "This isn't going to settle for $20,000. My client will never take it.
>
> Dan: "And why doesn't $20,000 seem fair?"

Dan's not going to settle this case for $20,000. But that's okay. At least he isn't talking about $100,000 for the next 45 minutes. And by the way, the longer he can get Mr. Steely to talk about wanting more than $20,000, the more that $100,000 figure is going to seem unreasonable to both of them.

Preparing Your Case

Many claims professionals can get nervous when they are about to negotiate with a tough adversary, an attorney, someone who knows a lot about the case or someone very experienced. Nerves can be battled effectively with the five P's – "prior preparation prevents poor performance". What great claims professionals know to do is to prepare. In this chapter, we introduce you to the process great negotiators use to thoroughly prepare their argument in a way that will convince the other side what is said is meaningful to them and persuade them over to their point of view.

The "So What?" Test

The first step is to write out the strengths and the weaknesses of the case to capture all the facts. You may do this in all your negotiations. We have seen some great claims adjusters take the time to write out the strengths and weaknesses, really focus on those facts, especially the strengths they established. However, when it comes time to actually present those strengths and weaknesses, they fall through a bit because they didn't take the extra step that really great negotiators know you always have to do. What is the extra step? It is the "So what?" test and it can help you with every case you handle.

You might handle other types of claims but since most of us can relate to cars, we will learn how this works by observing claims adjuster, James, handle an auto related accident. James captures the following notes as he prepares for his negotiation with the attorney, Lauren, on a liability case where he is looking to settle the injury claim.

Strength - There was very little damage to the rear bumper of the claimant's vehicle.
Strength - They didn't start treating for twenty five days after the initial loss.
Strength - They had a pre-existing injury that will help settle the case for the low end of the range.
Weakness – Insured was intoxicated
Weakness - Insured left the scene of the accident

James is excited about the strengths of the case as he makes the call to Lauren:

James: "So, Lauren, your client was injured, but I have to tell you, there really wasn't much damage to the rear bumper of your client's vehicle."

Lauren: "Yeah, so what?"

James: "Well... he probably wasn't going very fast."

Lauren: "Oh yeah, so what?"

James: "Well....how could he have been injured?"

Lauren: "He just was."

When James presented his argument, "There really wasn't much damage to the rear bumper," is that really what he meant to say? No. What he really meant to say was, "Your client probably couldn't have been injured in this accident because the damage wasn't significant to the car." Great negotiators say what they mean to say. If you have a point to make, make it.

Let's take another look at James negotiating with Lauren as he argues what he thinks is another strength of the case:

James: "Lauren, I have to tell you, your client didn't start treating for 25 days after the initial loss."

Lauren: "Umm... so what?"

James: "Well, I mean, there was a delay in treatment."

Lauren: "Uh...so what?"

James: "Well, I don't see why there was a delay in treatment. I mean, the claim must not be worth as much."

James is doing all the talking here and still not making his points. When James says, "There was a delay in treatment", what he was really trying to say is, "Your client must not have been that injured in this accident or they would have gone to the doctor right away." or "If your client was really injured, they would have started treatment prior to twenty five days after the accident."

If you have a point, make it!

In our case scenario, Lauren is responding "so what?" and we won't hear that in a typical negotiation. Lauren's responses to what James thinks are case strengths that demonstrate how the "So what?" test can be applied as you devise your arguments in cases you negotiate. When you plan what you are going to say when you bring up a strengths of a case, ask yourself "So what?" The answer to "So what?" is the real point you are trying to make.

Now that James has the "so what" test at his disposal, let's give him another chance to use two strengths and see if he will be more effective in the way he presents them to Lauren:

> *James: "Lauren, now I've got to tell you, there was very little damage to the rear bumper of your client's vehicle, which tells me he can't be as injured as he claims. Also, he took 25 days to go to the doctor, so I don't really believe he could have been hurt that badly. So, based on that information..."*

There is much more impact when James says what he really means. Maybe, just maybe, Lauren will say, "you've got a point."

Addressing the Weaknesses

Now that we have learned how to take that extra step in preparing the strengths of your cases, let's learn how to overcome the weaknesses.

It's important to remember, when you're presenting the strengths and weaknesses, you are in a conversation. As we learned in chapters 12 and 13, you want to stay in your conversation, not slip into the other person's conversation. Whose conversation is the strengths? The strengths are your conversation. Whose conversation is the weaknesses? The weaknesses are the other person's conversation. You have to do a really good job of staying in your conversation.

We know that great negotiators never argue with reasons – they argue the facts. Even though the weaknesses are facts, great negotiators don't spend a lot of time arguing about them. If the other person says, "Your client was drunk", a great negotiator will not say, "Well, yeah, but he was only a little drunk", and start arguing. If the other side gives you the reasons, and you begin to argue with them, guess whose conversation you're in? You're in their conversation.

One practice to help you stay in your conversation is to visualize that the facts are a conversation and the weaknesses are just a distraction. Great negotiators anticipate the weakness, treat it as a distraction and move the conversation back to the strengths of the case. They look for ways to minimize the weaknesses, and get back to talking about the strengths.

For the example here, minimizing the weakness and getting back to the strength would be to say, "Yes, our insured was intoxicated. But that doesn't make your client any more injured. What I want to discuss is why it took your client 25 days to go to the doctor." In your preparation, you anticipated addressing that the insured was intoxicated; you don't argue that obvious weakness in the case, you minimize the weakness, and get back to the strength, staying in your conversation.

Another weakness of this case is being a hit and run. When the other party says, "Your client hit mine and took off", you would not argue that fact by responding, "Well, he had a good reason for leaving." In your preparation you would have anticipated addressing that the insured left the scene and would be prepared to respond, "Yes, you are right the insured did hit your client and take off. He felt so bad about that, he turned himself in the same day. None of that changes the fact there is hardly any damage to your client's car. Based on that fact, there's no way your client was injured in this accident." This response does not argue weaknesses; it treats the weakness as a distraction, gets you back to the strength, staying in your conversation.

This process is not easy but it is possible. The process is proven by great negotiators. In the next chapter, you get a case scenario to practice what you have learned.

Practice Preparing an Argument

Here is an opportunity to use a case scenario and practice what you would actually say when presenting an argument to the other side. You will capture the strengths and weaknesses of the sample case. For the strengths of the case, apply the "So what?" test, and write out your argument to really bring your point home with the other side. For the weaknesses of the case, write out what you're going to say to minimize the weakness and get back to the strength. Practicing with a sample case will help you when you do this with your next true case negotiation. See Figure 16.1 on how to prepare your table for your argument statements.

B. I. AUTO CASE SCENARIO

On May 2, Matt Hall drove his new Mercedes Benz from home to the other side of town for his weekly chiropractor appointment, which he had been going to for three months due to a back strain he received at work. Our insured, Drew Brees, was on his way to renew his driver's license which had lapsed on April 30th, and rear-ended Mr. Hall as they were both driving down Canal St.

> It is certainly an inconvenience being in an accident, but Matt was relieved the rear bumper showed little damage. Matt took the car to a repair shop and was pleased it only cost $1,800 to have the damage repaired. Matt hired attorney Morris Bart because of his severe back pain. On May 23rd, Mr. Hall went in for back surgery.

Even for those of you who are not familiar with auto accident cases, you can probably identify a couple of strengths and weaknesses from the insurance company point of view.

On a blank piece of paper prepare a table like you see in Figure 16.1. In the "Strength" box, list the points you would like to bring up to the attorney. In the "How you will say it" box, write down word for word what you would actually say to the attorney in bringing up the strength. Be sure what you say passes the "so what" test.

In the "weakness" box, list the points you can imagine the attorney bringing up to you. In the "How you will respond" box, write down word for word what you would actually say to the attorney to minimize the weaknesses and get back to your strengths.

Figure 16.1

STRENGTH	HOW YOU WILL SAY IT

WEAKNESS	HOW YOU WILL RESPOND

CHAPTER 17

CASE SCENARIO ARGUMENT REVIEW

How did you do preparing your argument? Finding the strengths and weaknesses in this case was probably easy for you. Did you use the extra step of applying the "So what?" test and minimizing the weakness to get back to the strength to really bring your point all the way home? Writing effective arguments to say what you mean and influence the other side is a great exercise to build your skill. Compare the following suggestions to your own argument statements:

STRENGTH	HOW YOU WILL SAY IT
Low visible damage to the bumper	*"There was very low impact to the rear of your client's vehicle. That probably means the impact wasn't significant to cause the injury we see here."*
Pre-existing treatment	*"Your client was already being treated for his prior back injury. At worst, we may have aggravated the injury a bit, therefore it's extremely unlikely that this accident had anything to do with his need for back surgery. Therefore, we really don't owe you for those damages."*

WEAKNESS	HOW YOU WILL RESPOND
Liability 100% to insured Attorney says: *"My client was minding his own business when your insured callously slammed into him."*	*"We have already accepted liability, so let's move on to discussing the value of this case and how there is hardly any damage to either vehicle indicating a very light impact."*
$1,800 damage to vehicle Attorney says: *"This was a severe impact, my client's car had $1,800 worth of damages."*	*"Yes, there was $1,800 damage to your client's car. But a $90,000 car is an expensive vehicle. And it was just to fix a scratch on the bumper. What we need to do is get back to the fact that there was hardly any impact to this vehicle and I'm concerned how Mr. Hall could even be this injured."*

WEAKNESS	HOW YOU WILL RESPOND
Back surgery needed Attorney says: *"My poor suffering client had to have surgery after your insured plowed into him!"*	*"Mr. Hall did have surgery three weeks after the accident, but he was already being treated for this exact injury when the accident happened. Therefore, it's very likely that this was just an extension of that injury and the accident didn't cause it at all. Let's go back to discussing his treatment prior to the accident."*
Suspended driver's license Attorney says: *"Your reckless insured was driving around with a suspended driver's license. That is not going to look good to a jury."*	*"Actually, his license had expired, it was not suspended. But, really, that has nothing to do with the fact that this is the third time your client has claimed injury to his back, and was in fact currently receiving chiropractor treatments. We need to get back to the important issue at hand."*

Whether you handle workers comp claims, general liability claims, auto claims, farm claims, inland marine claims, or another type of claim, take the time and use this process to prepare for your negotiations. Your job is stressful enough without negotiating your cases on the fly. Prior preparation of your argument is the key to effectively persuading the other side.

Here is one for you PIP adjusters:

PIP CASE SCENARIO
On September 1, your insured Ms. Lady Gaga, just after receiving her 74th tattoo, decided to go out to celebrate with her good friend, Katy Perry, a renowned psychologist.   Dressed in their best daisy duke outfits, Lady and Katy jumped in Lady's Yugo and headed off Just like they did last Friday night for some dressin' up and fireworks. Just as Katy was telling Lady about some teenage dreams she had been having, they were viciously rear-ended by a Mini Cooper traveling at a blistering 18 mph.

The driver of the Mini Cooper was none other than the brilliant rocket scientist, Brittney Spears, Ph.D. Seems Dr. Spears was slightly distracted due to shaving her head while driving. Although Dr. Spears denied doing anything wrong, she was overheard calling her lawyer and saying, "Oops, I did it again".

Although there was some damage to both vehicles, the airbags were not deployed. Further, there were no injuries reported at the scene, no ambulance called, and no one taken to the hospital. Lady just had a little lipstick smeared across her poker face.

A full two and a half months later, however, on December 17, both Ms. Perry and Ms. Gaga reported injuries and sought treatment.

Ms. Gaga complained of soft tissue neck, back and shoulder pain. She sought treatment at the famous Witch and Gypsy clinic, and treated with the highly sought after specialist Dr. Stevie.

Ms. Gaga treated daily for the first two weeks, and then three times per week for four additional weeks. The bills total $20,225. Per the fee schedule, Ms. Gaga is still owed $12,752. The remaining policy limit is $7,978.74. Ms. Gaga wants all the doctors at the clinic to wear meat uniforms, but Dr. Stevie nixes the idea.

Katy Perry also sought treatment with Dr. Stevie at the Witch and Gypsy clinic, complaining of neck and back pain, with similar treatment pattern and bills totaling $20,465. Per the fee schedule, Ms. Perry is still owed $13,137.10.

> On January 3, you received the IME report from the distinguished Dr. Jessica Simpson, which showed no positive findings. You stopped making payments at that time. You have paid $2,170.64 and $2,021.25.
>
> The provider wants $8,000. You have no history of negotiating with them. Your evaluation of the file indicates a range of $4,000 to $6,000, including what you have already paid.

On a blank piece of paper once again prepare a table like you see in Figure 16.1. In the "Strength" box, list the points you would like to bring up to the attorney. In the "How you will say it" box, write down word for word what you would actually say to the attorney in bringing up the strength. Be sure what you say passes the "so what" test.

In the "weakness" box, list the points you can imagine the attorney bringing up to you. In the "How you will respond" box, write down word for word what you would actually say to the attorney to minimize the weaknesses and get back to your strengths.

Here is one for you Workers' Comp adjusters:

W/C CASE SCENARIO

After seven years in Tibet, Brad Pitt returned to the U.S. to snatch a job as a dishwasher for seven dollars an hour at The Favor, the Mexican restaurant on Babel Ave. and Abby Singer Dr. in Cool World, Kalifornia. It was located across the tracks from the tree of life near the moneyball factory.

Brad worked at The Favor for 1 year beginning in June, and claims to have a cumulative trauma injury to his back, knees, hands and eyes. He also claims injury to his thumb when he got a burn after reading the safety manual for the new dishwashing machine, and he even claimed injury to his two happy feet when it fell on him during installation.

According to Sinbad, the manager at The Favor, Brad quit working not because of any injury, but because he was confronted by the owners, Mr. & Mrs. Smith, about playing Spy Game on his cell phone all day, and showing up late and intoxicated after attending meetings at his 'fight club'.

Co-workers Thelma & Louise, who seem happy together, say they saw no evidence of any injuries at all, especially none from his job duties. They say he used to leave work in good spirits to meet Joe Black on the way to their fight club. They say they knew Brad back when he got in trouble for cutting class in high school.

Other than a DME prescription from Dr. Johnny Suede and a full frontal lumbar spine MRI report from Dr. Jolie, you have not received any medical reports. Current medical treatment status is unavailable. Presently, there are no immediate medical-legal examinations scheduled.

Brad is represented by attorney Troy Megamind, who is known to have a mighty heart for his clients. Upon Mr. Megamind's request, the DWC Medical Unit has issued Qualified Medical Evaluator panels in the fields of Pain Medicine and Ophthalmology.

Brad was scheduled to give a deposition, which you were to use to extensively explore medical treatment (both related and unrelated to this alleged injury, in the present as well as the past), but he never showed up. It has been reset but not yet taken place.

The return to work status is currently unclear. However, it was known that Brad had concurrent employment with another restaurant called Legends of the Fall, which he thought was pretty neat because a river runs through it.

Brad is currently not receiving any compensation as the claim is denied.

Supplemental Evaluation Information:

Brad's life expectancy is 37 years.

You did insure for entire CT.

The paid Comp breakdown is: $185 for Claimant Legal expenses.

The EDD rate of pay is $185 a week, and the potential is $9,620 (52 weeks).

The findings of the MRI were: degenerative changes 1 to 2 mm at L3-4; L4-5; L5; S1

A Tens unit was prescribed.

There was not any activity check investigation to see if he's still working other jobs.

There was AOE/COE investigation.

Subrosa has not been done.

The lien amounts are: EDD $9,620; Claimant Legal $585 and Pacific Interpreting $260.

His average weekly earnings were $200 from this employer.

The TD and PD rates are both $133.33.

It is unknown how long Brad worked for other employer.

There is no written documentation of the disciplinary action taken by employer.

On a blank piece of paper once again prepare a table like you see in Figure 16.1. In the "Strength" box, list the points you would like to bring up to the attorney. In the "How you will say it" box, write down word for word what you would actually say to the attorney in bringing up the strength. Be sure what you say passes the "so what" test.

In the "weakness" box, list the points you can imagine the attorney bringing up to you. In the "How you will respond" box, write down word for word what you would actually say to the attorney to minimize the weaknesses and get back to your strengths.

Even though you are on your way to being a great negotiator, in the next chapter, we are taking your skill up yet another notch.

Just for fun, how many Brad Pitt movies were mentioned in that W/C case scenario? Only count each movie once, even if mentioned more than once. Answer at the end of chapter 21.

CHAPTER 18

STAY FOCUSED ON YOUR GOAL

In this chapter, we share several additional elements to keep you focused when you're preparing to negotiate. You will write these into your arguments, with your goal being to effectively influence the other side without searching for information or details during the conversation.

Negotiation Strategy

The negotiation strategy is a one line sentence that summarizes the overall strengths of the case. This negotiation strategy is your theme to live by, it keeps you hitting hard on the points you want to make. Great negotiators tell us that developing this one line strategy reminds them of the true strengths of their case and keeps them focused. Write out your negotiation strategy as you study your case and prepare your arguments for negotiation.

Given the prior case you just worked on, a negotiation strategy might be:

"Avoid liability and focus on low impact and prior injury"

Great negotiators develop a negotiation strategy to effectively stay focused during their negotiations. They take the time to write out in advance, their negotiation strategy, what they want to learn during the negotiation and what they are willing to reveal and make them a part of their negotiation conversation.

Up to this point, you have learned some tools on how to negotiate for cooperation, how to overcome objections, and how to avoid the Claims Hammer. You have learned the five steps in negotiating a settlement. Now it's time to really talk about the settlement amount. How do you effectively use your negotiation range to get to the resolution for a reasonable amount?

CHAPTER 19

USING YOUR NEGOTIATION RANGE

A common mistake even skilled adjusters make when negotiating claims is not having a set plan for how they want to use their negotiation range.

While monitoring calls, we have heard adjusters come up with $500, and then in the next conversation, they come up another $500, then another $500 in the next conversation, on and on. If you take this "level increase" approach, the other side really has no idea where you want to end up with this claim. All they know is, "Cool! Every time I talk to this adjuster, they go up $500!" You know what's going to happen? They're going to start calling you five times a day and you are going to get to a very high number very, very quickly.

Another common pitfall we hear adjusters make when using their negotiation range is called the "sporadic pattern". This is where there's really no rhyme or reason on how they increase their offers. They might increase it $100 now, $1,000 later, $700 in the next conversation, $1,500 in the next. With this pattern, the other side, again, has no idea where you want to end up. Without that understanding, they are less likely to come down within your range any time soon.

Increasing in Diminishing Amounts

The approach we suggest you consider is called "increasing your offer in diminishing amounts". The key is having your preset low to high range, and analyzing where your next offer will be before you pick up the phone. This takes a lot of the anxiety, and the frustration out of your negotiations. As you increase your offers, for whatever reason you see fit, based on their movement, arguments that are made, you're increasing your next amount in a smaller increment than the last. For instance, you're not going to increase as in the "level increase" example or in the "sporadic pattern" example above. You will increase your figure by $1,000 first, then the next increase would be $750, the next $500, and $250 after that.

What this approach does is set the expectation in the mind of the individual you're negotiating with, that you are out of money. Whether it's an attorney, or an unrepresented party, they clearly see you working to settle this claim and can comprehend where that number is going to be. It plants a seed that you are not increasing to any unrealistic numbers they might be hoping for.

This is a very effective approach and takes some practice. Consider you are negotiating a claim and have a range of $10,000 to $14,000. In the space below, write your next three offers. Remember, $10,000 is your starting point and you go up by smaller amounts each time you make a new offer. The key is planning ahead, giving care not to exceed your high range as your total.

$10,000	$	$	$	= $	Not to exceed $14,000 total

Were you able to come up with three incremental offers that diminished in their amounts as you proceeded in the negotiation, and total less than $14,000? If you decided on $2,000 the first time, $1,000 the next and $700 the last, you executed this negotiation tool successfully. Try this in your next negotiation; just remember the key is to plan ahead!

CHAPTER 20

FREQUENTLY ASKED QUESTIONS

To conclude, we would like to share answers to the most frequently asked questions we receive during negotiation classes. Some of the questions are already covered in this book; treat those as a review.

1) Is it a good idea to ask the other person how much they want?

Generally, it is not a good idea to ask the other person how much they want. If you do, you're implying that what they want changes the value of the claim. It also implies that you and the other person are on the same level. Remember, you are the expert, you have the experience and you have the knowledge.

Imagine you are going to have a surgical procedure. How would you react if the doctor said to you, "*Well, we need to remove this out of your body; Do you think we should go through your chest or do you think we should go through your back?"*? How would that make you feel? Would you respond, *"You're the expert, Doctor, why don't you know?"* It is the same thing as you asking the other person what they think it is worth or how much they want.

If the other person tells you what they want, which happens frequently, that is fine. You don't need to prove them wrong. You want to get back to your figure and explain why it's right, staying in your conversation.

2) Should we always insist on getting a demand package from an attorney before we make an offer?

This question is almost like question #1. Remember, you want to stay in your conversation. If you insist on getting a demand before you make the offer, you're giving them first chance of staying in their conversation. As a matter of fact, you are anchoring the beginning of the conversation in their demand.

Some attorneys are going to send you a demand package and there's nothing you can do about it. If they do, you might just ignore their figure since you have your information and you know why you're right. You don't need a number from an attorney to get started.

What you insist on is getting the information, the medical bills, and all the documentation. You are better off without a demand amount from an attorney.

3) Is it a good idea to tell the other party we have full authority to settle the case?

This is a great question that relates to the "opening statement". We think it is positive to tell the customer or other party you have full authority to settle the case. You aren't telling them you have policy limits authority and you aren't mentioning your range – you don't want to do that.

To tell them you have full authority to settle the case means they don't have to go over your head to your supervisor, they can deal with you. It means if you decide something they say means you shouldn't even make them an offer, you can make that decision. It means if you decide after you make an offer that you want to rescind it, you have authority to do that. This is all positive.

4) Do you think people might get annoyed if I ask them "why"?

Most people want to be understood. It is very hard to understand where people are coming from if you don't at least ask them why. The key is asking with a positive tone. Most customers will appreciate the fact that you asked them "why". That's your trigger to demonstrate you understand their point of view.

5) Is it a good idea to tell people I have 20 years experience?

The point of telling them that is to reassure them. You might say, *"I've been doing this for over 20 years and I'm going to do what I can to make sure you are fairly compensated."* You would not use your years of experience to "pull rank", as with, *"I've been doing this for over 20 years so what do you know?"* Use your experience to build trust not to attack or demean people.

6) Do I really want to tell the other person we want to be fair to all parties or fair to both parties?

Yes. We like telling the person that we want to be fair to everybody. Tell them your main goal is to make sure they are fairly compensated and we also have our insured to consider, the policy and the law. "We want to be fair to all parties" lets them know there are other considerations.

7) Should I tell people my main goal is to make sure they are fairly compensated?

This goes with question #6. Yes, tell them. So many customers start off thinking our main goal is to cheat them. We like to let them know, my main goal is to make sure you are fairly compensated. Why? Because, if you have done a really good job of showing them you've done the leg work, you've done your homework in the case, you've made concessions, they may just believe the statement that your goal is to make sure they are fairly compensated. This builds trust, and they may just trust your figures.

8) If I get an outrageously high demand from an attorney, do I respond with a real low-ball offer?

That's an easy one and the answer is no. You're the claims professional and you have a fiduciary duty to treat people right. Even if the person is represented, they are still a customer and you have to do the right thing. The best thing to do is treat it like it's not even a real demand and just begin your offer within your range like you were going to anyway.

CHAPTER 21

FINAL THOUGHTS

The very best negotiators we have known are ones that remember that claims is a customer service business. It is not our job to pay the least amount we can. Our job is to pay a fair and equitable amount, and help our customers understand we are fulfilling the promise we made to them.

Thank you for learning with us. You now have the same processes, tools, techniques and skills used by the very best claims negotiators.

We hope you can use these to improve your negotiation outcomes.

(Answer to Brad Pitt question: 27)

Professional Speaking Services

Carl Van is a professional national speaker having delivered presentations throughout the U.S., Canada and the U.K.

His presentation style is upbeat, fast paced and always generates audience participation. He has received numerous recognitions throughout the years, including Most Dynamic Speaker at the national ACE conference.

Mr. Van is qualified to speak on virtually any subject regarding employee performance and customer interaction. Just a few of his Guest Speaking titles include:

General
- Awesome Claims Customer Service: You're Good. You Can Get Better
- How to Avoid Losing Customers
- The Claims Customer Service Standards: 5 Things to Never Forget
- Practical Claims Negotiations: Stop Arguing and Start Agreeing
- Real Life Time Management for Claims
- Stress Management: Give Yourself a Break Before You Die

- Improving your Attitude and Initiative
- Getting People's Cooperation – A Few Easy Steps
- What Customers Hate – And Why We Do It
- If You Can't Say it Simply and Clearly, Then You Don't Know What You're Talking About: Some Business Writing Basics
- Empathy: The Power Tool of Customer Service
- Why Are They Calling Me? Things to do to Reduce Nuisance Calls
- Let Me Do My Job: Simple Steps to get People to be Patient and Let You Do Your Job
- Trust Me: Effective Ways to Gain Credibility
- Saying No: The Right Way (and easy way), or The Wrong Way (the hard way)
- Claims Listening Skills: How to Avoid Missing the Point
- Teamwork for Claims: Ways to Reduce the Work Created by Individualism

Management
- Handling Your Difficult Employees (Without Threats and Violence)
- Teaching and Coaching for Claims Supervisors and Managers

- Initiative: How to Develop it in Your Staff
- Stop Wasting Your Time – Practical Time Management for Managers
- Effective Delegation: Why People Hate It When You Delegate, and How to Change That
- Managing Change
- Interviewing and Hiring Exceptional Claims Performers
- Motivating Your Team
- How to Make Sure Your Employees get the Most out of Training
- Inspiring Employees to Improve Themselves

For a free DVD, please visit www.CarlVan.org or call 504-393-4570.

"Like" Carl Van on www.Facebook.com/CarlVanSpeaker for updates.

Follow Carl Van on www.Twitter.com/CarlVanSpeaker

In-Person Training Services

Carl Van is President & CEO of International Insurance Institute, Inc. that delivers high quality claims training directly to customers at their locations. He is the author of over 75 technical and soft skill courses that have been delivered to over 100,000 employees throughout the U.S, Canada and the U.K. Just a few titles of his programs include:

Employee Soft-Skill

- Real-Life Time Management for Claims
- The 8 Characteristics of the Awesome Adjuster
- Claims Negotiation Training
- Conflict Resolution
- Awesome Claims Customer Service
- Managing the Telephone
- Attitude & Initiative Training for the Employee
- Empathy & Listening Skills for Claims
- Employee Organization – Managing the Desk
- Prepare for Promotion – Employee Leadership Training
- Teamwork Basics – No Employee is an Island
- Interpersonal Skills – Improving Team Member Relations

- Effective Recorded Statements
- Business Writing Skills for Employees
- Beating Anxiety and Dealing with Anger – Help for the New Employee

Manager Soft-Skill

- Time Management for Claims Supervisors and Managers
- Coaching and Teaching for Claims Supervisors and Managers
- Keys to Effective Presentations
- Teaching Your Employees the 8 Characteristics of Awesome Employees
- Motivating Your Team
- Handling Difficult Employees
- The New Supervisor
- Interviewing and Hiring Exceptional Claims Performers
- Delegation Training for Supervisors and Managers
- Managing Change
- Team Training
- Leadership Skills for Claims Supervisors and Managers
- Preparing Effective Performance Appraisals
- Managing the Highly Technical Employee

For more information and a free catalog of courses, please visit www.InsuranceInstitute.com or call 504-393-4570.

On-Line Training Services

Carl Van is President and owner of Claims Education On Line website that delivers high quality claims training through streaming video that employees can access anywhere in the world.

He is also available to write, direct and present training courses specific to an individual company or industry. He wrote and presented a claims customer service course on DVD for a national company which was rolled out to all 18,000 line employees.

He is the designer, author and presenter of four on-line claims video training courses:

- Exceptional Claims Customer Service
- Negotiation Skills for the Claims Professional
- Real-Life Time Management for Claims
- Critical Thinking for Claims

For more information, visit www.ClaimsEducation OnLine.com.

Educational Articles by Carl Van

Carl Van is owner and publisher of Claims Education Magazine, and is the author of numerous articles that have appeared in various periodicals.

Just a sample of articles written by Carl Van:

Van, Carl. "The Claims World Loses One of Its Best: Mike Noakes." Claims Education Magazine www.Claims EducationMagazine.com. Winter, 2012

Van, Carl. "Oh, Her? She's New: A Lesson in Attitude and Performance." Claims Education Magazine. Winter 2011

Van, Carl. "A Lesson in Attitude and Performance." Skin Inc. November 2011

Van, Carl. "Saying 'No' the Right Way." Looking Fit. www. LookingFit.com. May, 2011

Van, Carl. "3 Maxims for Successful Negotiation." HVACR Business. May 2011

Van, Carl. "How to Say No the Right Way." OTC Beauty Magazine. July 2011

Van, Carl. "Gaining Cooperation Three Maxims for Successful Negotiation." The Industry Source. July/August 2011

Van, Carl "Negotiation – Understanding the Other Point of View." Promotional Consultant Today. www.promotional consultanttoday.org April, 2011

Van, Carl "Gaining Cooperation."
The Minnesota News, June, 2011. Pg. 13.
Sales and Service Excellence Magazine, May, 2011, Pg. 12.
InSite Magazine. May/June, 2011, Vol. 25, No. 6, pg. 10.
Audiology Advance Magazine. www.audiology.advance web.com April, 2011
Pharmacy Week. www.pharmacyweek.com April, 2011
Print Wear Magazine. www.printwearmag.com April, 2011
The Real Estate Professional Magazine. www.therealestatepro.com April, 2011

Weekly Article Magazine. www.WeeklyArticle.com March 2011.

Industrial Supply Magazine. www.industrialsupply magazine.com March, 2011.

Furniture World Magazine. www.Furninfo.com March 2011.

Contact Professional. www.ContactProfessional.com March 2011.

Promotional Consultants Today. www.Promotional ConsultantToday.org; March, 2011.

Van, Carl "Three Maxims for Successful Negotiation." Dealer Marketing Magazine www.DealerMarketing.com March 2011.

Van, Carl. "Our Life's Work." Property Casualty 360. www. PropertyCasualty360.com January, 2011.

Van, Carl. "The Five Standards of Great Claims Organizations." Property Casualty 360. www.PropertyCasualty360.com February, 2011.

Van, Carl. "Online Claims Training Program Expands: Time Management for Claims added to curriculum." Claims Education Magazine. www.claimseducationmagazine.com Fall 2010.

Van, Carl. "5th Annual Claims Education Conference Earns Superbowl Status." Claims Education Magazine. Summer 2010: Pg. 1.

Van, Carl. "While Others Wait, Bold Companies Invest in Training." Subrogator. Winter 2010: Pg. 102.

Van, Carl. "While Others Wait, Bold Companies Invest in Training Part III." Claims Education Magazine. Spring 2010: Pg. 1.

Van, Carl. "Claims Education Conference and the Superbowl Champs." Claims Education Magazine. Spring 2010

Van, Carl. "Customer Service and the Claims Professional." Claims. December 2010

Van, Carl. "A New Season Awaits." Property Casualty 360°. July 2009

Van, Carl. "Welcome to Our Launch." Property Casualty 360°. July 2009

Van, Carl. "While Others Wait, Bold Companies Invest in Training Part II." Claims Education Magazine. December 2009- Vol. 6, No. 6: Pg. 1.

Van, Carl. "While Others Wait, Some Invest in Training." Claims Education Magazine. October/November 2009- Vol. 6, No. 5: Pg. 3

Van, Carl. "Tips on Taking Statements & Information Gathering." Claims Education Magazine. October/November 2009- Vol. 6, No. 5: Pg. 1.

Van, Carl. "Hiring and Motivating the Right People." NASP Daily News. November 2009

Van, Carl. "Placing the Bets." Claims Education Magazine. March/April 2009- Vol. 6, No. 2: Pg. 1.

Van, Carl. "Lessons in Customer Service & Attitude." Claims Education Magazine. January/February 2009- Vol. 6, No. 1: Pg. 1.

Van, Carl. "Saying It the Right Way." Claims Education Magazine. Fall 2008- Vol. 5, No. 4: Pg. 8.

Van, Carl. "Critical Thinking Part Three." Claims Education Magazine. Summer 2008- Vol. 5, No. 3: Pg. 4.

Van, Carl. "Critical Thinking Part Two." Claims Education Magazine. Spring 2008- Vol. 5, No. 2: Pg. 4.

Van, Carl. "Critical Thinking Part One." Claims Education Magazine. Winter 2008- Vol. 5, No. 1: Pg. 4.

Van, Carl. "Desire for Excellence." Claims Education Magazine. Fall 2007- Vol. 4, No. 4: Pg. 14.

Van, Carl. "Above All Else: There is Attitude." Claims Education Magazine. Winter 2006

Van, Carl, "Meeting the Challenges of Time Management." Claims Education Magazine. Summer 2006

Van, Carl. "Building a Claim Team." Claims. October 2005.

Van, Carl. "In Search of Initiative." Claims. September 2005.

Van, Carl. "A Velvet Hammer Can Expedite Negotiations." Claims Education Magazine. Summer 2005- Vol. 1, No. 1: Pg. 10.

Van, Carl. "Claims Management: Desire for Excellence." Claims. July 2005.

Van, Carl. "Empathizing with Customers." Claims. June 2005.

Van, Carl. "Never Stop Learning." Claims. May 2005.

Van, Carl. "Interpersonal Skills: Avoid the Hammer." Claims. April 2005.

Van, Carl. "Secrets of Successful Time Management." Claims. March 2005.

Van, Carl. "Attitude." Claims Magazine. February 2005: Pg. 10.

Van, Carl. "Secrets of Successful Time Management." Claims Magazine. March 2005

Van, Carl. "Adjusters Can Steer Clear of Headaches by Avoiding the Hammer." Claims Education Magazine. Summer 2005

Van, Carl. "Tend to Your Garden: A Vision of Claims Education." <u>Claims.</u> February 2003: Pg. 34.

Van, Carl. "Adjusters: How not to Drive Away Clients." <u>National Underwriter</u>. September 24, 2001.

Van, Carl. "Adjusters Should Holster 'The Hammer'." <u>National Underwriter</u>. November 2001

Van, Carl & Sue Tarrach. "The 8 Characteristics of Awesome Adjusters." <u>Claims.</u> December 1996.

Carl Van is available for consulting, training and guest speaking appearances. To contact Mr. Van, call 504-393-4570 or visit:

www.CarlVan.org
www.Facebook.com/CarlVanSpeaker
www.Linkedin.com/CarlVan (Carl Van - Awesome Adjuster group)

Articles Featuring Carl Van

Mr. Van has been the subject of numerous articles outlining his services and educational philosophy. A few are:

Staff. "Customer Service Fundamentals." <u>Canadian Insurance Top Broker</u>, Feb. 6, 2013

Meckbach, Greg. "Claims Managers Must Remember Importance of Customer Service." <u>Canadian Underwriter, Daily News</u>. Feb. 6, 2013

DeWitt, Margaret. "Make Sure Your Reps Understand That Their Job is Helping Customers." <u>The Customer Communicator</u>. September 2011

DeWitt, Margaret. "Does Your Attitude Toward Your Job Need Adjusting?" <u>The Customer Communicator</u>. September, 2011

Couretas, Catherine. "Maximize Your Employee Training, Performance." <u>International Association of Special Investigation Units</u>. September 2011

Bramlet, Christina. "Speaking of Gaining Cooperation with Carl Van."

Claims. April 2011, Vol. 59, pg. 8.

Property Casualty 360. www.PropertyCasualty360. com. April, 2011

Gilkey, Eric. "Strategies for Gaining Cooperation." IASIU. Monday, September 13, 2010: Pg. 4.

Henry, Susan, and Mary Anne Medina. "Evaluating Adjuster Performance." Claims. August 2010: Pg. 36.

Gilkey, Eric. "Hiring and Motivating the Right People." NASP Daily News, November 3, 2009: Pg. 6.

Gilkey, Eric. "Ace Awards: Most Dynamic Speaker." Claims. July, 2009, Vol. 57, No. 57, Pg. 6.

"Permission to Say, 'I'm Sorry'." Canadian Underwriter. September 1, 2008.

Aznoff, Dan. "Fair Oaks Students Take Speaker's Advice to Heart for Positive Attitude." The Sacramento Bee. April 12, 2007: City Section, Pg. G5.

Friedman, Sam. "WC Claimants 'Not the Enemy,' Trainer says." National Underwriter. September 24, 2001.

Prochaska, Paul. "Awesome Adjusting Revisited: A Return to Customer Service." Claims. February, 2000.

Hays, Daniel. "Being Kinder and Gentler Pays Off: Insurance Claims is a Customer Service Business." <u>Claims.</u> December 2000: Pg. 56.

Carl Van is available for consulting, training and guest speaking appearances. To contact Mr. Van, call 504-393-4570 or visit:

www.CarlVan.org
www.Facebook.com/CarlVanSpeaker
www.Linkedin.com/CarlVan (Carl Van - Awesome Adjuster group)

Additional Books by Carl Van

Van, Carl. The 8 Characteristics of the Awesome Adjuster. Published by Arthur Hardy Enterprises, Inc., ISBN 0-930892-66-6 (Metairie, LA) Copyright © 2005

Van, Carl. Gaining Cooperation: Some Simple Steps to Getting Customers to do What You Want Them to do. Published by International Insurance Institute, Inc., ISBN 1456334107 & 13-9781456334109 (New Orleans, LA) Copyright © 2011

Van, Carl. Attitude, Ability and the 80-20 Rule. Published by International Insurance Institute, Inc., ISBN 1461052947 & 13:9781461052944 (New Orleans, LA) Copyright © 2011

Van, Carl and Hinz, Debra. Gaining Cooperation: 3 Easy Steps to Getting Injured Workers to do What you Want Them to do. Published by International Insurance Institute, Inc., ISBN: 1461104009 & 13:9781461104001 (New Orleans, LA) Copyright © 2011

Van, Carl and Wimsatt, Laura. The Claims Cookbook: A Culinary Guide to Job Satisfaction. Published by International Insurance Institute, Inc., ISBN: 1460976657 & 13:9781460976654 (New Orleans, LA) Copyright © 2011

Van, Carl. The Eight Characteristics of the Awesome Employee: Published Pelican Publishing ISBN: 978-1-4556-1734-0 & 978-1-4556-1735-7 (Gretna, LA) Copyright © 2012

Carl Van is available for consulting, training and guest speaking appearances. To contact Mr. Van, call 504-393-4570 or visit:

www.CarlVan.org
www.Facebook.com/CarlVanSpeaker
www.Linkedin.com/CarlVan (Carl Van - Awesome Adjuster group)

Contact Carl Van

Carl Van is available for consulting, training and guest speaking appearances. To contact Mr. Van, call 504-393-4570 or find him at any of the following:

www.InsuranceInstitute.com

www.ClaimsEducationConference.com

www.CarlVan.org

www.ClaimsEducationMagazine.com

www.Facebook.com/CarlVanSpeaker

www.ClaimsEducationOnLine.com

www.Twitter.com/CarlVanSpeaker

www.ClaimsProfessionalBooks.com

www.Linkedin.com (Carl Van – Awesome Adjuster group)

www.YouTube.com/CarlVanTV

www.CarlVanClaimsExpert.wordpress.com